P9-DCL-727

A Devotional Guide to LUKE

The Gospel of Contagious Joy

Other Books by John Killinger

A Sense of His Presence. The Devotional Commentary: Matthew
His Power in You. The Devotional Commentary: Mark
Bread for the Wilderness, Wine for the Journey: The Miracle of Prayer and Meditation
All You Lonely People, All You Lovely People
For God's Sake, Be Human
The Centrality of Preaching in the Total Task of the Ministry
Hemingway and the Dead Gods
The Failure of Theology in Modern Literature
World in Collapse: The Vision of Absurd Drama
Leave It to the Spirit: Freedom and Commitment in the New Liturgy
The Salvation Tree
The Fragile Presence: Transcendence in Modern Literature
Experimental Preaching
The Second Coming of the Church
The 11:00 O'Clock News and Other Experimental Sermons

The Word Not Bound: A One-Act Play

A Devotional Guide to LUKE

The Gospel of Contagious Joy

John Killinger

WORD BOOKS
PUBLISHER
WACO, TEXAS

A Devotional Guide to Luke: The Gospel of Contagious Joy

Printed in the United States of America
Library of Congress catalog card number: 79-67670
ISBN 0-8499-0257-6

Scripture quotations marked KJV are from the King James or Authorized Version of the Bible.

Scripture quotations marked P are the author's paraphrase.

Contents

Introduction

Most people, if pressed to say which of the four Gospels in the New Testament is their favorite, would probably answer that it is the Gospel of Luke. Matthew contains the Sermon on the Mount, with its beautifully phrased Beatitudes. Brief little Mark is full of miracle narratives and sayings about being able to "see" with one's eyes. John talks grandly of eternal life and the "many mansions" in the Father's house—passages of great comfort often read at funerals. But Luke, more than any other Gospel, is the Gospel of stories.

There are the popular Christmas stories about the angel's visits to Zechariah and Mary, the birth of the child in the stable, and the lowly shepherds who heard heavenly choirs singing "Glory to God in the highest." There is the unforgettable tale of the good Samaritan—probably the most haunting picture ever given to mankind of what it means to be a neighbor. There are the three ever popular stories of the lost sheep, the lost coin, and the lost boy. There is the sobering narrative of the rich man and Lazarus. And there is that long, inspiring resurrection story of Jesus' walk with the two disciples on the road to Emmaus.

It is hard to imagine the history of Christian faith and its preaching without these incredibly pictorial stories. Yet not one of them appears in any Gospel but Luke's.

There is something else unique about Luke. It is the only Gospel whose author wrote a sequel, a companion-volume about the history of the early church. That is what the Book of Acts is—a companion-volume to Luke. This means that Luke is the only Gospel whose language, structure, and theology we can interpret in the light of another book written by the same author. You may not have thought about it before, but this can be extremely important in trying to understand some of the more obscure sayings in an ancient manuscript. It is certainly very helpful in the case of Luke.

We know very little about Luke himself, as we know little of the other Gospel writers. Tradition holds that he was the doctor whom Paul mentioned in Colossians 4:14, Philemon 24, and 2 Timothy 4:11 as his traveling companion. There is no strong evidence against this tradition and the language of medical knowledge in both the Gospel and Acts would seem to corroborate it.

Luke's being a doctor might indeed account for the strong humanitarian flavor of his writings. More than any other Gospel, his emphasizes God's care for the crippled and rejected members of society. From the song of the angels to the poor, semireligious shepherds on the hillsides (Luke 2:8–20) to Jesus' promise of Paradise to the criminal next to him at the crucifixion (Luke 23:42–43); from the Master's announcement in Nazareth that his ministry was for the poor, sick, and oppressed (Luke 4:14–30) to his controversial decision to dine with Zacchaeus, the outcast tax collector (Luke 19:1–10), the unfailing orientation of the Gospel is toward the weak, the lost, and the despised.

Luke may also have been sympathetic toward the rejected people of Jesus' environment because he himself was a Gentile writing for a Gentile audience. Both the Gospel and Acts were addressed to a certain Theophilus, whom Luke called "most excellent," possibly indicating that he held a position of eminence in the Roman government.

Rome had taken a very hostile attitude toward Christians since A.D. 64, when Nero unjustly accused them of burning the city. Luke was probably attempting to present their case in a more favorable light by retelling their story from the beginning through the missionary advances made in the years after Jesus' death. He was concerned to show both that Christianity was the true fulfillment of Old Testament religion and that it was the contentious old Judaizers, not the members of the Christian movement, who were the real rabble-rousers and troublemakers. Jesus' Kingdom, Luke tried to demonstrate, was never meant to replace the rule of Caesar; it was a transcendent, spiritual Kingdom, aimed at restoring dignity and hope to the poor and neglected. The Jewish elders had misunderstood this and, against Pilate's wishes, had insisted on Jesus' crucifixion. Even as he had gone to his death, Jesus had warned the people of Jerusalem that their foolishness would bring reprisals from Rome (Luke 23:27–31).

Far from counseling sedition and revolution, Luke maintained, Jesus had spoken to the people of joy and devotion. If there is a single tonal theme uniting the entire Gospel and the Book of Acts, in fact, it is the note of great joy that came to the people with the birth of Jesus. Over and over again, Luke used the words *joy*, *great joy*, and *rejoicing*. The angels' song reverberates throughout his writing, as the very heavens themselves resound with excitement at what is taking place in Jesus' ministry and the work of the early church.

Perhaps this fact, together with the unforgettable stories we have alluded to, accounts for the perennial appeal exercised by the Gospel of Luke. In a day of instant communication, when we are continuously depressed by the news of a world in general distress, it is wonderful to be able to turn to a Gospel like this that begins with a miraculous birth during a tax enrollment and ends with the crucified Christ walking the roads with his disciples and making their disillusioned hearts burn again with hope.

If you yourself are ever bothered by disillusionment, there is nothing better you can do in the next twelve weeks than spend a few minutes a day reading through this Gospel, meditating on the commentary in this book, and then waiting quietly in prayer before God. It cannot fail to affect your attitude toward yourself, your disposition toward others, and your understanding of what it means to be a follower of Jesus.

I must emphasize the importance of *listening* as you read. It is not enough merely to race through the words, repeating them.

The meaning is often in the silences, the gaps between words and sentences. It is there that the "still, small voice" comes to speak to us, in accents known only to the heart. It is there that we hear the real note of joy, there that we feel the call to discipleship, there that the world is changed for us.

So wait and listen—and you will not be disappointed.

JOHN KILLINGER

WEEK 1

Week 1: Sunday

Luke 1:1–4 A Definitive Account

"Every biographer and historian," says the essayist Northrup James, "attempts to write the best account yet. Drawing on all that has gone before him, yet adding that unique quality which he alone can give, he seeks to say the definitive word, the one that will marshal all the others into gleaming perspective. Even though additional writers may come after him, assaying the same task, his story, he hopes, will provide the unavoidable focus for theirs."

This must have been the feeling of Luke as he began his account of the life of Jesus and the early church. Many others, he said, had already written their accounts. But he wanted to write his, putting it together with his own unique touch.

Theophilus, to whom both the Gospel and the Book of Acts are addressed, may have been a well-to-do patron or benefactor of Luke, as suggested by the courteous form of address. His name, which means "beloved of God," could indicate that he was born of Christian parents and was younger than Luke. If this is the case, then the Gospel and Acts were written by Luke as an effort to lay before his young friend the salient facts of the early Christian movement as he had received them from both eyewitness reports and the writings of others who were ministers or servants of the Word. Theophilus had already heard reports of the origins and progress of the movement; but Luke wished him to have a very careful account and to "know the truth."

Lord, thank you for the men and women in the past who have cared enough for the truth to write reports about matters for those of us who would come after them. Help me to cherish their efforts and to ponder their accounts for the meaning they have in my own life. Then help me to love my children and their children and their children's children enough to pass on to them my own testimony on these things. For your kingdom's sake. Amen.

Week 1: Monday

Luke 1:5–25 Starting with the Temple

Luke significantly begins his Gospel in the temple. Mark began with the story of John along the banks of the Jordan River, and Matthew commenced with the genealogy of Jesus. But Luke is thinking of the account of the Christian movement he will write in the Book of Acts; with its center in Jerusalem, it will surge outward to the Greco-Roman world the way ripples travel outward from an epicenter. In other words, Luke sees with a *spatial* vision, even when writing history. Therefore he begins his account in the temple, which for centuries has been at the heart of God's dealings with Israel. A Gentile himself, he is interested in the way the gospel of the Kingdom has reached the nations. But the story necessarily starts in Jerusalem.

It begins with Zechariah, the elderly priest who was to father

John the Baptist. As a male member of the tribe of Aaron, Zechariah was entitled to offer sacrifice in the temple. But there were so many descendants of Aaron that they were divided into groups which served in the temple only two weeks each year. Within each group, lots were cast to decide which priest would be permitted to officiate. No priest was allowed to do this more than once in a lifetime, and even then many never had the opportunity. We can imagine Zechariah's excitement, therefore, when the lot fell to him "to enter the temple of the Lord and burn incense." He must have trembled in anticipation. He would burn the incense representing the prayers of the people while the crowds of people stood outside. It was a supreme honor—enough even to offset the sense of shame Zechariah had felt at having had no child.

Then it happened! As the prayers of the people were being offered, an angel appeared to Zechariah in the midst of the smoke from the incense. God would answer both the prayers of the people for deliverance and Zechariah's prayer for a son. The son's name would be John. He would take the ascetic vows of a Nazirite, and would go out "in the spirit and power of Elijah," who was regarded as the greatest of the prophets.

Zechariah could not believe it. Like so many of the Jews depicted later in the Gospel, he asked a sign of proof—and received a very personal one—he was struck speechless until the time of the birth! How the people must have talked that day when they went home about the priest who had seen a vision at the altar and was left dumb by the experience. But aren't all great mystical experiences finally unspeakable?

Lord, I have been speechless a few times in my life, but never like this. Lead me through prayer and contemplation to greater depths of spiritual experience, so that I talk less and hear more. Through him whose story is at the heart of this mystery. Amen.

Luke 1:26–38 The Greater Miracle

From the miracle of birth to the elderly, God now turns to the miracle of birth to an unmarried young woman. If John's birth was special, the Savior's birth must be even more special. He would be born as the offspring not of an old priest of the temple but of the Holy Spirit of God himself.

"Hail, Mary, full of grace," Jerome translated the Greek in the Latin Vulgate edition, and a tradition arose which venerated Mary as the receptacle of grace that could be dispensed to others. But the Revised Standard Version more properly translates, "Hail, O favored one, the Lord is with you!" It was indeed an incredible honor; she had been chosen to bear the Savior of the world.

Luke, with a touch of human understanding that is characteristic of him, shows us the puzzled, frightened side of Mary's reaction. She "was greatly troubled at the saying, and considered in her mind what sort of greeting this might be." The angel's answer to her thoughts was an assurance and a promise. It was the same promise the Jewish people had been concerned with for centuries—the promise of an eternal King to sit on the throne of David—and this time the promise involved Mary herself, as the mother of this King. Verse 35 is a beautifully reserved description of how the conception would occur. The birth would be the fulfillment of ages of national hope and expectation.

I like what Professor G. B. Caird of Oxford has written about this. For Luke, he says, the special sense in which Jesus was "the Son of the Most High" was only the starting point. "As the Gospel proceeds, we shall see Jesus taking this inherited notion and remodelling it in the crucible of his own experience. He spoke of God as 'my Father' and of himself as 'the Son,' not to expound a doctrine or to claim a rank but to express his own personal relationship to God, whom he knew intimately as only a son can know a father."

Meanwhile, Mary's final response to the angel was one of astonished modesty and humility: "Behold, I am the handmaid of the Lord; let it be to me according to your word."

Lord, this story is liable to seem fanciful and untrue in the kind of world we live in today. Yet you still send your word to those you favor, and your Holy Spirit upon those who are devout in their own spirits. Teach me to say, "Let it be to me according to your word," that I may know your will in my life, and submit to it in similar humility. In the name of him whose Kingdom is forever. Amen.

Week 1: Wednesday

Luke 1:39–56 The Blessedness of Believing

This is a remarkable passage, especially in view of the low general estate of women in New Testament times. With continuing sensitivity, Luke describes the gentle, feminine side of this mighty event that was taking place in the history of Israel and the world.

What Luke attempts to do is to relate the later ministry of the Lord to the entire context of prophecy and expectancy in Israel's long history. God is working behind the scenes, so to speak, to coordinate the events that will finally culminate in the birth, death, and resurrection of a Savior.

Mary, in all of this, personifies the faithful remnant in Israel who persist in believing in the promises of God. As Elizabeth says, "Blessed is she who believed that there would be a fulfilment of what was spoken to her from the Lord" (v. 45).

The song attributed to Mary is called the *Magnificat*, which is the first word in the song's Latin version. It is a psalm of thanksgiving, very much like many of the poems in the Book of Psalms. It speaks of God's covenant-faithfulness; as God has chosen Mary over all the highborn ladies of the age to be the mother of the Savior, he is now ready to exalt the low, the poor, and the hungry over the high, the rich, and the well fed. As the psalm concludes, this is no new promise, but the fulfillment of the one made to Abraham long ago.

Luke does not say it directly, but he implies that Mary remained with Elizabeth until Elizabeth delivered her child. It would have been the kinlike thing to do, and three months should have brought them just about to that time. What wonders we can imagine the two women sharing during this period!

Lord, fulfillment must have been hard for these people to wait on, and then hard to believe when it was almost upon them. Strengthen my faith in the promises you have given us, that I too may live in the blessedness of believing. Through Jesus, who is the fulfillment. Amen.

Week 1: Thursday

Luke 1:57–80 The Gracious Gift of God

Here, especially in verse 65, we are given a clue about where Luke got these stories that are not told in the other Gospels. They circulated among the people in the little hill communities near Judea, where John was born. Luke apparently heard them from Christians in this region.

Like the other stories, this one provides interesting personal details whose ultimate meanings reflect universal truths. Zechariah's and Elizabeth's neighbors came to rejoice with them at the birth of their son and to be present for his ritual circumcision. At the moment in the rite when the child is to receive his name, the neighbors and kinfolk, assuming that the boy will be named for his father, proceed in the father's silence to name him. But Elizabeth speaks up to say that his name will be John, meaning "gracious gift of God." It is an understandable gesture, given the parents' elderly status. But the friends and kin brush Elizabeth's answer aside, deferring to Zechariah. They fully expect a sign from him confirming that the child should bear his name.

Zechariah startles them—twice. Writing on a tablet, he indicates that the child will indeed be called John, not Zechariah. Then he startles them again by suddenly regaining his voice. He begins to speak, and his first words are expressions of praise to God. The neighbors and kinfolk are filled with fear. They know that something far beyond the usual is going on here. They are dealing not with man but with God.

Given the gift of prophesying, Zechariah delivers a poetic utterance praising God and predicting that John will be the forerunner of the Lord himself, preparing his ways by calling people to repentance and forgiveness of their sins.

Lord, a birth is a sacred occasion, and so is receiving a name. Make me more aware of the sacredness of my own life, and let me know it is a gift from you. Through him who calls us to new life in your will. Amen.

Week 1: Friday

Luke 2:1–20 News of a Great Joy

In this passage, Luke revels in a major theme of his Gospel—the joy that is associated with Jesus and the Kingdom. Gabriel had promised "joy and gladness" to Zechariah (Luke 1:14). The babe in Elizabeth's womb leaps for joy at the visit of Mary (Luke 1:44), and Mary's psalm rejoices in God (Luke 1:74). When the seventy disciples return from their preaching mission, they announce with joy that even the demons are subject to them (Luke 10:17). Jesus tells them to rejoice that their names are written in heaven (Luke 10:20). He himself rejoices in the Holy Spirit (Luke 10:21), and then declares to them, "Blessed are the eyes which see what you see!" (Luke 10:23). After Jesus healed the woman bent with an infirmity, "all the people rejoiced at all the glorious things that were done by him" (Luke 13:17). And of course there are the three stories of joy in chapter 15, about the finding of the lost coin, the lost sheep, and the lost boy. Who can ever forget the loving father's glad cry when his boy returns: "Bring quickly the best robe, and put it on him; and put a ring on his hand, and shoes on his feet; and bring the fatted calf and kill it, and let us eat and make merry; for this my son was dead, and is alive again; he was lost, and is found" (Luke 15:22–24)? More than any other New Testament writer, Luke is captivated by the notion of joy, and the Gospel resounds with it.

Here, of course, is the central occasion for joy—the coming of the Savior in human flesh to inaugurate the long-awaited Kingdom. Appropriately, he is identified by birth with the poor, who have no place to lay their heads, and with the religious pariahs—the shepherds—who are socially despised by the religious rulers of Israel.

And the religious outcasts see the shining glory of the Lord's presence and hear the voice of an angel. "I bring you good news of a great joy," says the angel, "which will come to all the people" (v. 10). When the announcement is made, the whole sky is suddenly filled with the music of heavenly choirs, praising God and promising peace among those "with whom he is pleased!"

Peace is more than the absence of war, in this case; it is the Hebrew *shalom,* meaning fullness and blessedness. As for what it means to please God, we have but to remember the words of Luke 3:22, which were heard at Jesus' baptism: "Thou art my beloved Son; with thee I am well pleased." Jesus pleased the Father by being obedient to a baptism for repentance and forgiveness of sins.

Characteristically for Luke, the shepherds, having learned the joyful news, in turn become its bearers. They went back to the hills, "glorifying and praising God for all they had heard and seen" (v. 20). The joy of the kingdom is that contagious!

Lord, I am heartily sorry for the lack of joy in my life. I am too frequently tired, depressed, and annoyed. My life should be a continual paean of praise, for I have both heard and seen the coming of your eternal Kingdom. Forgive my tediousness. Restore to me the passion of your salvation, and let me bear joyful witness to others of your transforming power. Through Jesus, who took his place among the poor and rejected of the world. Amen.

Week 1: Saturday

Luke 2:21–39 The Reward for Waiting

Luke, being a Gentile, was apparently somewhat confused about the Jewish legal requirements following the birth of a firstborn son. There were three such requirements. The first was circumcision, to be performed eight days after birth. The second was the payment of five shekels as a redemption offering, to be made at any time after the first month. And the third was the purification of the mother, performed after forty days, to restore her from uncleanness to the privilege of public worship. Luke seems to have mixed the second and third requirements in this passage—though it is possible that one trip to the temple would have sufficed for both.

The important thing is not the accuracy of his knowledge of Jewish legal customs, however, but the witness of the two old people in the temple to the special mission of Jesus as Savior of the people. Simeon's prophecy, composed largely of allusions to Isaiah 40–55, is remarkable for two things: it forecasts the universal mission of Jesus (he is to be "a light for revelation to the Gentiles") and it predicts the stormy, uneasy nature of the mission, including the pain that will pierce the soul of Mary herself when Jesus is crucified. Anna's speech, on the other hand, seems to have been one only of thanksgiving and witness to the redemption of the Jews.

There is something very tender about this vignette. I wonder how we would regard Anna today if she spent most of her time fasting and praying in church. Probably we would dismiss her as a harmless old woman whose devotion has gone a bit far. But in the Jewish culture of Jesus' day, aged people were highly regarded for their wisdom and spirituality, and the testimony of these two elderly souls who had waited all their lives to see God's redemption was a great benediction on the future Savior.

One question nags us: Why did Joseph and Mary marvel at what was said about Jesus? Could it be that their understanding of his mission was not full in the beginning—that it had to grow even as ours does?

Lord, I wonder if I really understand what it means that Jesus is the Savior of the world. It is such a large concept, and the world seems so resistant to being saved. Help me to fast and pray as Anna did—to lead a life of disciplined devotion—in order that I may comprehend more fully in all my being what my mind already knows about Jesus. For your Kingdom's sake. Amen.

WEEK 2

Week 2: Sunday

Luke 2:40–52 A Sign of the Future

How eagerly some parents observe their children's abilities and activities in order to determine what their life's work may eventually be! "Doctor, lawyer, merchant, chief" is an old game based on this eagerness to know the future. Today it has been replaced by aptitude tests and counseling services designed to point young people in the most appropriate directions.

In this passage, Luke reveals the early direction taken by Jesus. At the age of twelve, like every Jewish boy, he became *bar mitzvah*, a son of the Law. It was—and still is—one of the most important occasions in a Jewish male's life. Probably it was in celebration of this that Mary and Joseph took the boy on a pilgrimage to Jerusalem for the annual Passover festival. They would have been in the holy city for an entire week.

The fact that Jesus was not with his parents when they began the journey home, and that they traveled for an entire day while supposing him to be with kinfolk or acquaintances, gives us a fascinating insight into the nature of his social environment as a youth. We normally think of his family as though it were a nuclear family like our own. But it was actually a large, extended family, in which the young people moved freely among aunts, uncles, cousins, and friends. Therefore his parents assumed quite naturally that he was in the Galilean caravan as it moved slowly northward.

Jesus was, in fact, in the temple, revealing his leaning toward a future rabbinical life. He gravitated toward the learned teachers the way some youngsters today incline toward newspaper offices, laboratories, or mechanical contraptions. And his agility in discussing the Law utterly astounded the rabbis. It was confirmation both to them and to him that he would one day be known as a famous rabbi.

When his mother reprimanded him for being thoughtless of her and other members of the family, he replied with a significant answer—they should have known they might find him in his Father's house. It is an important identification. Already he understood his place as Son of God. How seriously he took this the world had yet to know.

Mary, says Luke, pondered all these things in her heart. Apparently she was the source of this story, and it became part of the oral legend of Jesus kept alive among the Christian communities in the Judean hills.

Lord, grant to the children I know the sense of direction and inner identity that Jesus had by the time he was bar mitzvah. *And let Jesus himself stand at the center of where they are going with their lives. For his name's sake.* Amen.

Luke 3:1–14 No Hiding Place

Whatever image we may have of John the Baptist, it certainly isn't of a soft-soaper! He did not cajole the crowds with humor or sentimental language.

"You brood of vipers!" he called them—a nest of snakes. "Who warned you to flee from the wrath to come?" It is the picture of a family of snakes wriggling furiously to escape the advance of a raging fire or swirling flood. The wonder is that multitudes swarmed the river bank to hear so abusive a preacher.

But John had to be strong and decisive to fulfill the prophecy of Isaiah about the forerunner of the Messiah. Isaiah pictured him as predicting the leveling of mountains and raising of valleys, the straightening of crooked ways and the smoothing of rough paths. He saw the judgment that was coming on Israel and the world, and knew that there would be no hiding from that judgment. There would be no crevices or turns in the road where anyone might take refuge.

Many people recognized the authenticity of John's warning and asked what they must do to avert the disaster.

It is interesting that his answer is couched in terms of simple justice. People who have more property than they need are to divide with those who have none. Those who have food are to share with those who are hungry. Tax collectors are to do their duty but forego the often exorbitant fees they have been accustomed to extracting for personal use. Soldiers are to live simply and honestly, not using their positions to rob or to falsely accuse people of crimes and confiscate their property.

The injunctions are not different from those which Jesus will give later for citizens of the heavenly Kingdom. They imply a new orientation in life, a new spirit, so that God, not personal profit, becomes the center of the person's life.

And, interestingly, Luke sets his account of the great wilderness prophet into a universal context. He begins (v. 1) by locating John's ministry in the reign of Tiberius, the Roman emperor, and then names the local governor, tetrarch, and religious leaders. John's message of repentance and justice was not meant for the little land of Judah alone, but for the world!

Lord, am I part of the hills—or of the valleys? Do I have more than others? Then I too need to hear John's message and prepare the way of the Savior in my life by sharing what I have. Grant me the grace, imagination, and resoluteness acceptably to do this. In the name of the One who has come and is always coming. Amen.

Week 2: Tuesday

Luke 3:15–20 A Great Humility

Only persons with a special quality of inner assurance and self-identity are capable of true humility. I once knew such a person. He was a powerful man and controlled the affairs of many employees. Yet, in the presence of anyone who could do anything better than he could, he gracefully acknowledged the other person's ability. I once heard him, when accepting an honor, enthusiastically credit his superior in another city with the leadership and insight that were responsible for the honor.

John was obviously in touch with himself in this way. When people came to him asking if he were the Messiah, it must occasionally have been tempting to him to suggest that he was, or at least to wonder in his heart if indeed God was not preparing him for this great station. But he was apparently quite resolute on the matter, and pointed people instead to the One whose ministry would follow his.

"I baptize you with water," he said; but the One coming "will baptize you with the Holy Spirit and with fire" (v. 16).

As Luke was also the author of Acts, we cannot help associating this verse with the description of what occurred at Pentecost, when a sound "like the rush of a mighty wind" filled the house where the followers were, "tongues as of fire" rested on each of them, and the Holy Spirit welled up in them and they began to speak in other languages (Acts 2:1–4). John's followers had experienced baptism in water. So had Jesus' disciples. But the *real* baptism, the one that would be the sure sign of the Kingdom's presence, would be the baptism of the Spirit and the fire, and that was the baptism Christ would bring.

John the Baptist, as Karl Barth has said, was content to be a signpost pointing the way to Jesus.

Lord, make me a signpost too. Let the joy of my spirit and the helpfulness of my actions point others unmistakably to Jesus, who stands at the center of everything. Amen.

Week 2: Wednesday

Luke 3:21–38 A Great Moment

There is no tenderer moment in a parent's life than the one when his or her child undergoes a rite of initiation or passage. A baptism, a confirmation, first communion, *bar mitzvah*, graduation, marriage—each is a time of deep and satisfying emotion, combining reflection on the past and anticipation of the future.

It is surely no wonder that the Gospel traditions represented God as speaking his delight at the moment when Jesus, his "only begotten Son" (John 3:16, KJV), was baptized by the prophet John. It is beside the point whether Jesus needed to be baptized "for the forgiveness of sins" (Luke 3:3); the important thing is that by accepting baptism from John he identified himself with penitent Israel, the Israel whose hope was still in the Lord. It was a sign of expectancy and obedience. Luke's way of putting it, "when Jesus also had been baptized and was praying" (v. 21), implies that the

Holy Spirit came to him in the form of a dove after he left the riverbank and was alone in contemplation. This seems less dramatic and improbable than the picture we have in both Mark and Matthew, where the Spirit descended immediately upon Jesus' leaving the water. Whenever it happened, at any rate, the Spirit's physical appearance was accompanied by a voice from God saying, "Thou art my beloved Son; with thee I am well pleased."

This is an interesting combination of scriptural quotations. The first, "Thou art my beloved Son," is from Psalm 2:7. Psalm 2 is a hymn exalting the king whom God has set over the nations to rule "with a rod of iron" and dash his enemies to pieces "like a potter's vessel." The second phrase, "in thee I am well pleased," is probably from Isaiah 42:1, in which God is speaking of his servant who will redeem Israel through the ministry of suffering and "bring forth justice to the nations." So the two motifs are combined—exaltation and suffering—and set at the very beginning of Jesus' ministry.

Then Luke gives a long genealogy, relating Jesus to David, the great king of Israel, to Abraham, the father of the Jews, and eventually to Adam and thence to God himself. The justification for placing the list of names here is the phrase "the son of God," which may be linked back to the voice saying, "Thou art my beloved Son." And by relating Jesus to Adam, as well as to David and Abraham, Luke underlines again his proclamation of Jesus as a universal Savior, not merely the Savior of the Jews.

Lord, the early church must have been thrilled by this picture of the Savior being baptized and hearing your voice as the Spirit descended on him like a dove. Help me to feel a similar excitement now as I contemplate the scene. Arouse in me a new enthusiasm for your Kingdom and for the leadership of your Holy Spirit in my own life. Through him who became a suffering King. Amen.

Luke 4:1–13 Trial in the Wilderness

"Thou art my beloved Son," God had said when Jesus was baptized. *"If* you are the Son of God," the devil says in two of the temptations recorded here. It was a challenge to Jesus' understanding of his identity—an attempt to get him to forsake the role of suffering servant God intended the Savior to take.

Each temptation was extremely basic to human nature.

The first was for *bread.* Jesus had been fasting for nearly six weeks, and was very hungry. Perhaps in his imagination the rounded stones of the barren foothills where he was meditating began to look like loaves of bread—luscious, hot loaves of bread fresh from the oven. "Go ahead," the devil invited. "Turn this stone into bread. You are the Son of God, aren't you?"

Jesus' reply is directly from the words of Moses in Deuteronomy 8:2–3: "And you shall remember all the way which the Lord your God has led you these forty years in the wilderness, that he might humble you, testing you to know what was in your heart, whether you would keep his commandments, or not. And he humbled you and let you hunger and fed you with manna, which you did not know, nor did your fathers know; that he might make you know that man does not live by bread alone, but that man lives by everything that proceeds out of the mouth of the Lord." The Israelites had spent forty years in the wilderness; perhaps it was for a symbolic reason that Jesus spent forty days here. In any case, the point is clearly made: as important as bread may seem, humble obedience to God is even more important.

The second temptation was to *power* and *glory.* The devil promised to make Jesus a great king if he would only fall down and worship the prince of darkness. According to famed psychoanalyst Karen Horney, this too is a temptation familiar to all mankind. In varying degrees, we all yearn for recognition and authority. If we are neurotic, it is the most basic drive in our make-up.

Again Jesus' reply is from the words of Moses: "You shall fear the Lord your God; you shall serve him, and swear by his name. You shall not go after other gods . . . for the Lord your God . . . is a jealous God" (Deut. 6:13–15).

The third and final temptation was *to put God to the test.* Whisked up to the top of the pinnacle on the temple porch, which rose to a height of 450 feet above the Gehinnom Valley at the base of Jerusalem, Jesus was urged to leap down. Psalm 91, after all, promised protection to God's chosen one; he could not be hurt, if indeed he *was* the chosen one.

How often we are tempted to put God on trial in our lives! "God, if you truly care, do this." "If you are really there, do that." But Jesus responded firmly, again from Scripture: "You shall not put the Lord your God to the test" (Deut. 6:16). Testing is God's prerogative, not ours.

In all three temptations—for bread, for glory, and for religious certainty—Jesus responded with the need for absolute obedience to God. What an important passage this must have been to early Christians who, for one reason or another, were tempted to defect from the faith! It places temptations squarely in eternal perspective—enduring them now in the wilderness of life leads eventually to the Kingdom which God alone can give.

> *Lord, I have too often forgotten the meaning of real obedience. This age knows far more about being free than about obeying. Yet it misses the first principle of freedom—that freedom is lost the minute one fails to obey you. Help me to discover again how to be faithful to the heavenly vision, and thus to be truly free. Through Jesus, who fulfilled this paradox magnificently.* Amen.

Week 2: Friday

Luke 4:14–30 The Design of Jesus' Ministry

Having flatly denied the devil's attempts to make him into a self-gratifying, power-hungry earthly king (Luke 4:1–13), Jesus now clearly denotes the kind of ministry he intends to pursue. It is to be a ministry to the poor and outcast, the blind and unaffirmed. And what happens when he announces his intentions signals the kind of reception he can expect from the religious Jews throughout the entire ministry.

Luke places the announcement of the servant ministry in a synagogue service in Nazareth. The synagogue was the heart of Jewish educational and religious life. A sabbath service in the synagogue usually consisted of a call to worship known as the *Shema* (Deut. 6:4–9), an assigned passage from the Law, a free passage from the prophets, a sermon, and assorted prayers. Any man in the synagogue, even a visitor, might be given a scroll and asked to read the Scripture or preach the sermon. The sermon was always preached from a seated position after the Scriptures had been read, and might be followed by questions from the audience.

On this occasion, Jesus was obviously invited to read the free selection from the prophets and then to provide the sermon. He chose Isaiah 61:1–2, which begins a long poem about the mission of God's mighty servant who is to restore Israel. When he announced that the long wait for the Scripture's fulfillment was at an end, the people were at first excited and pleased.

But then their doubts began to rear. This was Joseph's son talking. How could he hope to figure in the salvation of all Israel? Surely God would not use a hometown boy to save his people!

Some of the details of the conflict seem to be missing, and we must patch together what transpired. Apparently there was an exchange about the wonders Jesus had performed in Capernaum, another city to the north of Nazareth. But, as Mark informs us, he could do no mighty work in his hometown because of the people's disbelief (Mark 6:5–6).

Finally, in keeping with Luke's general emphasis on the worldwide mission of the Savior, Jesus went even further, and suggested that the Jews might entirely miss the great blessings of God. Israel had been full of widows in Elijah's day; yet Elijah went to the house of a widow in Sidon. Similarly, Israel had many lepers in Elisha's time; yet Elisha had given the blessing of God to a man from Syria.

The proud Jews could take no more! Touched to the quick, they rose up in anger and carried the brash young prophet out to throw him to his death, possibly on the charge that he had uttered blasphemy. Somehow, though—Luke does not trouble to be more specific—Jesus managed to walk through their midst and escape.

The tone of this entire passage is clearly an extension of that set by the temptation narrative. Jesus is faithful to the vision of God's will for his people, which calls for justice for the poor, the prisoners, the blind, and the oppressed. He will not swerve aside for anything—not to feed himself, not to gain personal glory, not to test God, and not to please the citizens of the town where he grew up!

Lord, how would I receive it if Jesus came into my life, as he did into these people's lives, upsetting the power balances and social structures within which I have learned to maneuver? I confess that I would probably feel as they did, and try to resist him. I know this means I am not fully converted to your Kingdom. Forgive me, Lord, and give me a humble spirit, that I may acquiesce in his vision and be saved. Amen.

Week 2: Saturday

Luke 4:31–44 Teaching and Preaching the Kingdom

In our day, we are prone to think of the teaching and preaching of the Kingdom primarily in terms of oral communication. Sometimes, as a professor of preaching in a theological seminary, I receive mail addressed to "The Professor of Speech."

But for Jesus, the Kingdom was coming in power, not mere talk. Therefore his teaching and preaching were interfused with miraculous acts of healing. When he announced in the synagogue at Nazareth (Luke 4:14–30) that he was anointed "to preach good news to the poor" and "to proclaim release to the captives and recovering of sight to the blind," he obviously had in mind far more than a mere announcement of the Kingdom's arrival. For him, teaching and preaching meant participating in the power of the new Kingdom! This passage (Luke 4:31–44), then, is the logical one to follow the declaration in 4:14–30. It shows the preacher of the Kingdom in action.

Luke seems to have taken over this particular collection of material almost verbatim from the Gospel of Mark (1:21–39), or from some source of stories available to both Mark and himself. About the only change he made in it is in the last verse (44), for which Mark reads, "And he went throughout all Galilee, preaching in their synagogues" (1:39). Luke does not mean to relocate the ministry by setting it in Judea, the territory to the south of Galilee. He uses the word Judea to denote all of Palestine (cf. Luke 1:5; 6:17; 7:17; 23:5).

The purpose of the selection in both Mark and Luke is to relate Jesus' healing ministry to the "authority" with which he taught and preached. When he spoke, it was not the carefully guarded speech of the scribes and Pharisees; it was the penetrating, free-moving discourse of one who was obviously in touch with his subject—and the miracles were simply further proof of this.

The demons recognized him as the true Son of God, and knew his coming shook their power and authority to the very depths. Their cries, as they left their victims, were filled with awe and respect: "You are the Son of God!" (v. 41). They realized that it was the beginning of the end for them. The scribes and Pharisees had never had any power over them. But they knew it was different with Jesus. He was "the Holy One of God," and his Kingdom's arrival meant the collapse of theirs.

Lord, I wonder if the demons did not show Jesus more respect than we often show him today. We sing "Oh, How I Love Jesus" and flash our bumper stickers with the message "Honk If You Love Jesus." Then we live as if he had not died for our sin and been raised as an eternal presence in our midst. It made more difference in the lives of the demons. They went away in hushed respect, forsaking even their dwelling places. Let him matter more to me, I pray, for his name's sake. Amen.

WEEK 3

Week 3: Sunday

Luke 5:1–11 An Astonishing Catch

What an encouraging story this must have been to the early church in times of frustration or despair!

The crowds had pressed Jesus right up to the water, trying to hear the Word of God about the Kingdom. As he talked, he saw the two boats come in empty from a night's fishing. The men in the boats tied up their vessels and began the arduous task of washing the leaves and algae out of their nets.

Getting into Simon Peter's boat, Jesus had him row out a short way from land and anchor there. Getting a little distance on the crowd in this manner, he was then able to sit down and teach from the boat. He probably did not preach uninterruptedly, as ministers usually do today, but answered questions as they came up, or even sat sometimes in silence, waiting for ideas to form into words or parables. And we can imagine Simon Peter, tired as he was from the night's fishing, waiting quietly in the boat and listening as Jesus talked.

Then, when he had finished speaking, Jesus turned his energies to his benefactor with the boat and the empty nets. "Launch out into the deep and let down your nets again," he said (v. 5, P). Simon started to protest, but thought better of it and obeyed. He and his men rowed out into the lake and dropped their nets again. How tired they must have been, and how useless this all seemed. But, to their utter amazement, the nets came in writhing and bulging with fish. There was such a catch that they had to signal the men in the other boat to come and help them, so the nets would not break, making them lose all the fish.

Peter's reaction is interesting. It was as if he had never before realized the holiness of the one he had heard teaching from his boat. Suddenly he was aware, and fell to his knees to worship. His words (v. 8) are reminiscent of those of Isaiah when he had a vision of God in the temple (Isa. 6:5). He had seen the Lord himself!

Jesus' words to Simon and the others were, "Do not be afraid"—further indication that they had recognized his holiness. They would be used in a special way in the Kingdom as fishers of men. So they obeyed their vision of his holiness by leaving their boats and homes to follow him.

Think how the early church would have heard this story. There must often have been periods when the Christians seemed to make no progress in converting the world regardless of how they had toiled. Then they would see this picture of Simon Peter, who became the head of the church, reluctantly rowing to deep water again and slowly letting out the great nets. They would envision the sudden churning of the waters as the nets were drawn up, with all the silver bellies flip-flopping in the air and spraying foam everywhere. What a lesson it was! They had but to listen for the voice and let down their nets at his bidding. He would give the church its increase.

Lord, I am often tired and lose faith when nothing seems to be happening in my life. Teach me to hear your voice at such times and to steer for the deep waters again. In the name of him who can keep the nets full. Amen.

Week 3: Monday

Luke 5:12–16 Release for a Captive

In the dialogue following his sermon at the synagogue in Nazareth, Jesus had alluded to Elisha's healing of the leper Naaman (Luke 4:27). Now he himself heals a man "full of leprosy."

Leprosy was one of the most dreaded diseases of that time, not only because of the way it wasted the body but because it isolated the victim socially and religiously. This man clearly became one of the "captives" referred to in Jesus' reading from Isaiah (Luke 4:18). According to Leviticus 13–14, which gave specific rules governing the leprous person, he was declared "unclean" by the priest and cast out from normal society.

Jesus is depicted as doing what most Jews would never do—he touched the leper, risking social and religious contamination for himself. But then the miracle occurred. Instead of his being contaminated by the leper, Jesus cleansed the man! He reversed the usual direction of effect, and opened a new future to the man!

Jesus' instruction to the man that he go to the priest and conform to the Levitical law and be pronounced well was probably for the man's sake socially—he would then be reintegrated into the normal fabric of Jewish society.

The verbs in the final sentences of the passage are interesting. They are all in the imperfect tense, denoting continuing activity. The word about Jesus *kept* going out; great crowds *kept* gathering to hear him and be healed; and he *kept* withdrawing and praying.

This is the picture we have seen in Matthew and Mark as well, of the dialectic between prayer and activity in Jesus' ministry. He constantly withdrew into solitary places to nourish his inner person through prayer and meditation. This, in turn, gave him unusual power in dealing with the great pressure of human needs and demands when he was among the crowds.

Lord, I am so guilty of forgetting this dialectic and trying to meet the demands of life without times of prayer and reflection. Please help me to see once and for all that I simply can't do it—that only the continued refreshment of your presence will enable me to deal adequately with the burden of busy days. Through Jesus, who fully understood this. Amen.

Week 3: Tuesday

Luke 5:17–26 A Characteristic Detail

The Pharisees were a special group of men who had separated themselves from normal pursuits in life to become guardians of the Law; hence their name, which means "the separated ones." The Law which they watched over was the Law of Moses plus the hair-splitting elaborations of each individual law within it; in other words, it was a very complex body of legalities. "Teachers of the law" was Luke's term for the scribes. These men specialized in interpretations of the Law, making them natural companions of the Pharisees.

The fact that Pharisees and teachers from all over Palestine had gathered to hear Jesus is an obvious sign of his growing fame and popularity.

As usual, Jesus seems to have been practicing a combined ministry of teaching and healing. Luke's word that "the power of the Lord was with him to heal" (v. 17) is one of the clearest indications in Scripture that this power was not always resident in Jesus himself but was a special gift from God. We can well imagine that the paralyzed man brought on a stretcher was not the only one who had come to Jesus borne by friends. But this one became the object of special attention because of the controversy with the scribes and Pharisees and the unusual manner of his entrance. Mark 2:4 pictures the man's friends removing part of the clay-and-wattle roof of a typical Palestinian home, but Luke provides the detail about removing the tiles (v. 19), indicating a Roman style of house.

The controversy arises over Jesus' first words to the paralyzed man, forgiving his sins. We are not certain why he spoke thus. Some commentators think he recognized the man's paralysis as a psychosomatic affliction; others, that he was underscoring the rootedness of illness and affliction in the presence of sin and evil in the world. I am inclined to the latter interpretation, and also believe that he ejaculated these words of forgiveness in celebration of the eagerness of the man's friends to bring him to Jesus by such an imaginative way. At any rate, the words released a torrent of questioning from the legalists present, who thought it blasphemous for any person to assume God's prerogative of pardoning iniquity.

Jesus' response is to show them something even more incredible—the restoration of the man's normal physical functioning. If they doubt his ability to forgive sin, then why is he given such power to perform visible miracles? They are all amazed and filled with awe, as if they have beheld sacred mysteries.

And Luke adds a characteristic detail omitted in Mark. He says the man who was healed went home "glorifying God." This is the note of joyous discovery that runs throughout the Gospel of Luke, from the announcement of the Savior's birth to the story of his resurrection.

Lord, I understand about Jesus' forgiving the man before healing him. I too am inwardly paralyzed by my sins and failures, and it is only as I feel your acceptance of me despite them that I begin to experience wholeness and joy. Then even my body feels better. Thank you, Lord. Hallelujah! Amen.

Luke 5:27–39 A New Mood of Rejoicing

At first glance, there appear to be two separate passages here, one about Levi and his friends, and the other about the question of fasting, amplified by the short parables of the garment and the wineskin. But one spirit pervades them both and makes a unity of them.

It has to do with the new kind of order that has come in Jesus. He is not a mere continuation of the old religious tradition represented by the scribes and Pharisees and their restrictive view of the Law. Instead, he brings an air of liberation, a fresh spirit of joy and celebration in life.

The people who have been cast away from the religious center because they could not keep the Law perfectly are brought back with joy (note the "great feast" in Levi's house), just as the prodigal son is received in the parable (Luke 15:20–24). And the disciples who follow the Master, themselves common, "unreligious" persons, likewise live joyfully instead of ascetically, celebrating their Lord's presence in their midst.

The brief parables of the garment and the wineskin, then, are metaphorical ways of saying that this exhilarating movement of Jesus cannot be merely appended to or enclosed in the traditional forms of religion; it is too dynamic, too volatile, and can only end by destroying the old way, as an unshrunken patch of cloth will do when sewn to a shrunken garment, or as active new wine will do when poured into old, dry skins.

Verse 39 appears only in Luke, and not in the parallel versions of Matthew and Mark. It seems to be a comment on those who find the old religion adequate—especially the scribes and Pharisees. They find the old wine to be good, so simply do not try the new wine. Jesus understood the difficulty of giving up old habits or traditions.

Lord, my problem is that I have allowed the "new" religion of Jesus and the disciples to become old in my life. My responses to you have become dull and routine, and I no longer have a continual sense of delight in my faith. Come as new wine in my life, tearing up old wine-skins; break me open to current joys in the Kingdom. For Jesus' sake—and mine. Amen.

Week 3: Thursday

Luke 6:1–11 The Priority of People over Traditions

This passage should be read as a continuation of Luke 5:27–39, for it is further commentary on what Jesus said there about the new mood of joy and excitement in the Kingdom. Fussiness about sabbath law was part of the strict religious tradition developed by the scribes and Pharisees. Jesus did not violate the Law of Moses, for he was a humble observer of divine law. But he certainly was not about to conform to the niggardly elaborations of that Law that had become such a web of bondage to observant Jews.

The first incident, plucking and eating grain on the sabbath, revolves about a regulation against milling corn on the holy day. It seems silly to us that rolling a few grains of wheat in one's hand to separate the kernels from the husks should be construed as milling or grinding, but that is the way the scribes and Pharisees had come to interpret it.

Jesus' answer to them on this score did not try to argue with the absurdity of their interpretation. Instead, it went to another "offense," one recorded in 1 Samuel 21:1–6 about David, who, with his men, had eaten the sacred bread of the Presence in the tabernacle. What this illustrated, as Jesus used it, was the priority of human need over any commandment. Thus the summation, "The Son of man is lord of the sabbath" (v. 5). It seems likely that Luke reported the phrase "Son of man" here as it was often used in the Old Testament (cf. Ps. 8:4), as merely a synonym for "man" and not as a messianic title. In other words, we do not have here a pronouncement about Jesus' lordship but a common-sense statement about the importance of human need when that need appears to contradict religious commandments.

The second incident, healing on the sabbath, defies the rule that a person could be doctored on the sabbath only if his life were in danger. Obviously this man's withered hand had not gotten that way overnight, and could await the following day for restoration. But again Jesus challenged the priority of the Law over human need by effecting the cure on the sabbath. What is more, he appears to have done it as an open affront to the legalists, because he invited the man to come and stand in the very center of the crowd as he performed the healing. It was a direct reflection of his declaration of ministry in Luke 4:16–30—healing the sick and releasing the captive were to have top priority in the Kingdom!

Verse 11 is a dark hint of what was to come. Those who cherished the old traditions could not bear to see them broken in this manner. They would eventually have their pound of flesh.

Lord, forbid that I should ever follow in the footsteps of the legalists by making any Christian *regulation more important than the people I meet in life. Fill my heart with such love and exultation that I shall never become defensive about mere traditions or habits of thinking. Through Jesus, who drew fresh dedication from everything.* Amen.

Week 3: Friday

Luke 6:12–19 The People of the New Spirit

Following his controversies with the religious leaders of Israel (Luke 5:17–6:11) and their rancorous discussion of what to do to him (Luke 6:11), Jesus appoints the twelve disciples who are to be the pillars of the new movement. The importance of the act is underlined by his spending the night praying in the hills. These are to be men whom God wants and who will be entrusted with the power to heal and to preach the Kingdom.

The number twelve is suggestive of the twelve tribes of Israel, indicating that the community of joyful celebrators gathered through the ministry of Jesus and the apostles would be the replacement for the moribund old Israel, which was too wrapped up in concerns for its regulations and traditions to fulfill the calling of God for a servant people to save the world.

With his newly appointed cabinet around him, Jesus then descends from the hills and meets the people "on a level place" to teach and heal them. This contrasts sharply with the picture in Matthew 5–7, where the "sermon" of Jesus is given on a mountain. Possibly the source from which both writers drew did not specify a place and each provided a different location from pure conjecture. Luke's basis for having the sermon on the plain would seem to be the pattern from Exodus 24, where Moses received the Law on the mountain but then descended before giving it to the people. Matthew, however, was concerned to represent Jesus as "a greater than Moses"; perhaps this led to his portraying Jesus as giving his sermon from the mountain instead of from the plain, indicating that he occupied a position higher than that of an intermediary, as Moses clearly was.

Regardless of what is intended by the place symbolism, Luke obviously emphasizes two things. First, the wide territory represented by the crowd that has gathered—it embraces all of Palestine and even the outlying districts of Tyre and Sidon. And, second, the continued connection of Jesus' activities with the program he announced in the synagogue in Nazareth (Luke 4:16–30)—he uses his power from God to effect healing for the sick and release for the captives.

Lord, Luke obviously intended to link Jesus' choice of his disciples with the ongoing work of healing and liberating people. How connected have these been in my own life? Have I too easily assumed that my discipleship has nothing to do with healing the hurts and illnesses of the people around me? Help me to ponder this and let you be Lord in my life the way you want to, not the way I think you should be. For your Kingdom's power. Amen.

Week 3: Saturday

Luke 6:20–31 A Sermon for the New Israel

Like Matthew's Sermon on the Mount (Matt. 5–7), Luke's Sermon on the Plain begins with the Beatitudes, describing the blessedness of those who are gathered up in the new Kingdom. This section forms a natural extension of Luke 4:16–30, in which Jesus defines his ministry as being to the poor, the sick, the outcast, and the oppressed. It is to these persons that the Kingdom belongs.

Thus the "woes" which follow in Luke's version (Matthew does not report any "woes" in the sermon) are most appropriate, for they are spoken rhetorically of all those who will miss the Kingdom because their riches, fine foods, present joys and respectability deafen them to the word of the gospel. Some commentators have conjectured that this section of "woes" was added to the text by the early church and was not really spoken by Jesus. But if we recall the extensive list of "woes" Jesus directed against the Pharisees in Matthew 23, we should not so readily question the authenticity of these "woes."

Matthew of course lists *nine* beatitudes, while Luke provides only four. And there is another notable difference in the two lists: Matthew has *spiritualized* his. That is, he has Jesus speak of "the poor in spirit" and those who "hunger and thirst after righteousness." Luke's Jesus, however, speaks of real poverty, real hunger, and real sorrow. The point he thus preserves is that God is going to look after the little ones of the earth; he is going to produce a great revolution in which the poor will receive what the rich have possessed. This is consistent with what John the Baptist predicted in Luke 3, that the high places would be brought low and the low places raised up, as well as with Jesus' sermon in the synagogue in Nazareth (Luke 4).

Running through this passage and the remainder of the sermon (vv. 32–49) is the note of intoxicating joy we have observed before in Luke. There will be great vexation among those who ignore the Kingdom's arrival, for they will lose everything. But the poor, the sick, and the oppressed will have reason for great rejoicing. They will eat and laugh at a great feast!

Lord, again I confess that my life is not joyful enough. Perhaps it is because I have too much, like the rich and the full in this section of "woes," or because I am shallow, like those who laugh now, or because I work too hard at being respected, like those who are well spoken of. These things crowd my mind and I cannot concentrate on you and the Kingdom. Forgive me, Lord, and lead me into a new level of consciousness where I shall know true blessedness. For your Kingdom is not only forever, but is here now. Amen.

WEEK 4

Week 4: Sunday

Luke 6:32–38 The Law of Love

This brief passage is Luke's equivalent of Paul's famous "love chapter," 1 Corinthians 13. It is set here in the Sermon on the Plain to indicate the absolute centrality of the loving spirit in the Kingdom of God.

To appreciate it fully, we must recall the ethic of the old Israel with which it contrasts. The heart of the Mosaic Law was the love of God and a careful adherence to the commandments. In practice, respect for the commandments had deteriorated into mere legalism—doing what was required of one and no more.

Jesus takes away nothing from loving God—in fact, on another occasion he says that loving God is the first commandment (Luke 10:25–28). But he seeks to avoid the spiritual and ethical impasse of the old legal system by describing those who are in the Kingdom as people who love and who therefore go beyond the requirements in their generous concern for others. They bless those who curse them, pray for those who abuse them, lend goods where there is little hope of return, and forgive those whom the Law would never forgive. In short, they are inwardly motivated to behave in a way that completely transcends the rule of law.

The genius of this way of life, of course, is that it rewards the person of the loving spirit with joy and peace that cannot be had on other terms. The person who keeps the Law faithfully may feel self-satisfied and righteous. But the one of the loving spirit feels something even better—an exuberance and sense of life akin to that of "the Most High" himself!

Lord, my mind has known the truths of these words for a long time, but I have forgotten them in my spirit. Rescue me, I pray, from the inadequacy of merely doing what is required, and give me the great joy of living selflessly, as you live. Through Jesus, who is a perfect example. Amen.

Week 4: Monday

Luke 6:39–49 Words for Disciples

Jesus had said that part of his ministry had to do with "recovering of sight to the blind" (Luke 4:18). While he meant this literally, it also had a great deal of figurative truth too, as we see from this passage. Being able to see matters clearly was regarded as essential in a disciple—otherwise Jesus' followers would produce the wrong kind of followers of their own.

If they had truly learned all they could from him, then they would produce good fruit, the way healthy trees do. They would be like a man who lays a solid foundation for his house, not like the one who is in haste to get his house up and so builds on the flat sandbar by the river without troubling to dig down and lay his foundation on the bedrock.

As Luke has arranged this material, it is an extended exhortation to thorough learning and discipleship, so that the follower of Jesus really becomes like his or her Master. Then the Kingdom will truly flourish in the world.

Lord, I am too prone to give you second-rate obedience instead of wholehearted discipleship. I am lazy about studying and learning what a follower of Jesus should know and practice in his or her life. I do not spend enough time each day in prayer and meditation. Help me to begin again and lay a better foundation before the floods of life come upon me and sweep away the little I have done. I want to see clearly and behave lovingly, for Jesus' sake. Amen.

Week 4: Tuesday

Luke 7:1–10 The Faith of a Foreigner

Luke has already ended his report of Jesus' Sermon on the Plain (Luke 6:20–49), but he may well have placed this story of the Roman centurion here as an illustration of the kind of life advocated by the sermon. The centurion is clearly a remarkable human being. Although technically an officer of the enemy occupation forces, he has behaved respectfully and lovingly toward the captive citizenry under his command. He has constructed a synagogue for their worship and educational needs, even though their religion differs vastly from his own, and has apparently shown his love for the people in other ways. When the elders from the synagogue come to bring Jesus to heal his slave who is very ill—probably a Jew who is a member of the synagogue—the centurion treats Jesus with the kind of respect normally reserved for kings and potentates. "I am not worthy of having you in my home," he says. "You can but say the word, and my servant will be healed." Beneath these humble words lay a great thoughtfulness. If Jesus were an orthodox Jew, entering the home of a foreigner would have been considered a defilement for him. The centurion probably expected that this was the case and wished to spare Jesus this transgression of his native custom.

"I tell you," exclaimed Jesus, "not even in Israel have I found such faith" (v. 9). The faith was obviously in Jesus' power to cure the man's slave. But it was also in a way of life which lay at the heart of Jesus' teaching: This centurion was a great example of the loving spirit of the Kingdom!

I saw a similar man once. He was a commanding officer in the U.S. Air Force. I went for a walk with him one day in Chieng Mai, a lovely town in Northern Thailand, and followed him into a Buddhist school and temple. He picked up the small children and loved them, and removed his shoes when he entered the temple, lest he offend an old man who sat watching us. Somehow he reminded me of the centurion in this passage. Jesus liked such people.

Lord, give me a loving spirit like this. Help me to see that the essence of true religion is in how I respond to the poor, weak, and oppressed of the world—not in how faultless I am about matters of religious dogma. Through Jesus, who lived this way himself. Amen.

Week 4: Wednesday

Luke 7:11–17 An Act of Compassion

This story of a dramatic resuscitation has rather clear theological import. Like Elijah in 1 Kings 17:17–24 and Elisha in 2 Kings 4:32–37, Jesus is seen as a prophet acting in the power of God to raise the dead. In this regard, the story serves as a preparation for the passage to follow, in which John the Baptist questions whether Jesus is the one "who is to come."

But Luke is obviously carried away in the telling by more than theological consideration. He is overwhelmed by the sheer human sentiment of it.

The picture is enough to bring tears to the eyes of the sternest of viewers. Jesus comes upon a funeral procession in a small town in Galilee. In the slow, mournful custom of the region, the procession winds through the narrow streets, led by the family, the professional weepers, and the coffin of the deceased. Apparently the poor widowed woman is in this case the only family member—all the others are friends. She will be left alone in the world—a terrible lot for an older woman in that culture—for she is burying her lone child.

It is a stark drama that greets Jesus as he arrives upon the scene—the mourning clothes, the loud wails of lamentation, the sight of the single woman accompanying the casket through the street. This is precisely the kind of setting he has said the Kingdom addresses.

"Do not weep," he comforts the mother.

He puts his hand upon the coffin—considered a defilement in traditional religion—and stops the procession.

"Get up, young man," he says. And the young man does.

It would be impossible to describe accurately the scene that follows. The people are jubilant—not merely because their friend's son has been raised from the dead, but because God has sent "a great prophet" into their midst! Small wonder that the "report concerning him" spreads like a windswept fire in dry grass to all the surrounding regions.

Lord, help me not to balk at the miracle of this story by asking if it really happened. Instead, let it speak movingly to my heart of the faith in which I am grasped, for there is truth that lies beyond the truth of my logical mind. Amen.

Luke 7:18–35 The Very Best Proof

In the narrative about the births of John and Jesus, Luke recorded how the baby John leaped for joy in his mother's womb when Mary came to visit Elizabeth (Luke 1:44). Here is a more realistic picture from adult life. Unlike Matthew, Luke reported no special recognition from John when Jesus was baptized. We are left to conjecture that the realization that Jesus was the promised Savior only began to dawn on John as he heard from his prison cell continued reports of the amazing ministry of Jesus.

When the men come from John seeking verification of Jesus' role, he gives them the best proof available. They observe as he heals the sick and restores the sight of the blind. "Go and tell John what you have seen with your own eyes," says Jesus—and he summarizes what they have beheld again in terms reminiscent of his declared program in Luke 4:16–30.

When the men have gone, Jesus ruminates about John and says what a great figure he has been. But he quickly adds that even the least of his followers who has seen the Kingdom is greater than John. It is Luke's way of emphasizing that John was the last of the old order and Jesus the beginning of the new.

Jesus' commendation of John apparently pleases many in the crowd who were disciples of John, but it raises murmurs of dissent among the scribes and Pharisees, who had been unwilling to accept the baptism of repentance. Noting the latter, Jesus muses about those who hold back and are unwilling to be caught up in a renewal movement. They are like children who hang about the marketplace—perhaps Jesus is watching some as he speaks—and complain that others will not do things their way. They did not like John because he was too strict and ascetic, and they do not like Jesus because he is too free and uninhibited in both his actions and his relationships.

The last word, "Yet wisdom is justified by all her children," is probably a proverb expressing a spirit of tolerance. We would say, "It takes all kinds to make a world."

Lord, I am often as fickle as the scribes and Pharisees, liking in one person what I dislike in another. Give me a heart of compassion, I pray, that I may accept even my enemies in prayer and thanksgiving. Through Jesus, who forgave from his cross. Amen.

Week 4: Friday

Luke 7:36–50 A Lesson in Joy

This passage may well be placed here as a further example of Jesus' knowledge of people and compassion for them. First there was the centurion whose slave was ill (Luke 7:1–10); then the widow whose son had died (Luke 7:11–17); then John the Baptist (Luke 7:18–23); then the crowds who heard Jesus speak about John (Luke 7:24–35). Now we see how Jesus treats a known prostitute and the Pharisee to whose home she comes.

We can only speculate, of course, but it was probably a daring thing for Simon the Pharisee to invite Jesus into his home, especially after the remark Jesus made in Luke 7:34 about his reputation as "a glutton and a drunkard, a friend of tax collectors and sinners!" The man should have known, as a strictly orthodox Jew who observed all the table commandments and house commandments, that he was asking for trouble. Still, we know from the fact that he did not provide the usual courtesies to Jesus—the foot bath, the kiss of greeting, the oil or perfume—that he was at least uncertain about his guest and how to receive him. Perhaps he invited him out of mere curiosity.

Apparently the men were reclining in the Roman manner, with their shoulders to the table and their feet behind them, and the woman simply approached Jesus in the courtyard or through an open door without his seeing her. Before she could get her flask of ointment open to anoint him, she began weeping, so that her tears fell upon his feet. Overcome by emotion, she loosened her long hair (as no proper woman would have done) and began wiping the tears with her hair.

Simon was inwardly outraged, and Jesus could doubtless see it in his face. Perhaps with genuine compassion for Simon, and not as a rebuke, Jesus told him the parable of the two debtors and then applied it to the present situation. The nameless woman was like the debtor who had been forgiven a king's ransom—she had much to celebrate and be grateful for. Simon, on the other hand, had had no such upheavals in his life. He was a man of careful behavior and suspicious nature. He did not know how to love and rejoice as she did.

We don't know the woman's motivation; it is not clear. There is a similar story in Mark 14:3–9 about a woman of Bethany who came into the house of Simon the leper and anointed Jesus' head in anticipation of his death and burial; John 12:1–8 identifies this as Mary, the sister of Lazarus, and again indicates it is for his burial, but changes the story to an anointing of the feet. Luke is possibly drawing on the same story, but uses it to proclaim Jesus' compassion, not his death and burial. In this version, he defends the woman against the unfriendly attitude of Simon the Pharisee and tells her that her sin—the behavior that has cut her off from "decent" society—is forgiven.

Thus Luke closes the five tales of compassion as he began them. In the first, Jesus commended a foreign centurion for having more faith than he had seen among the Israelites; in the last, he commends an obvious sinner, telling her, "Your faith has saved you." Luke's picture is clear—Jesus is forming the new Israel, the community of the redeemed, out of people summarily rejected by the legalists of the old Israel.

Thank you, Lord, for the grace of this story. I am more like Simon than the woman. Help me to see that my sin is as great as hers, and therefore my forgiveness even more to be prized. Through him who said we should celebrate whenever we have the bridegroom with us. Amen.

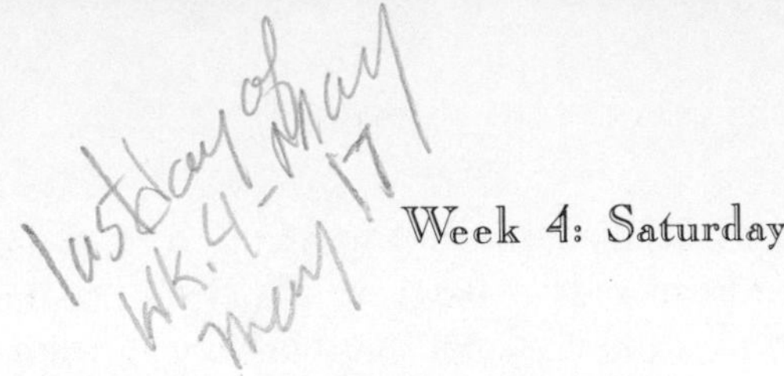

Luke 8:1–21 The Sower Goes Out

At this point in the Gospel, Luke represents Jesus as leaving the synagogue setting and moving more actively through the countryside, stopping in villages and cities along the way. He is like the sower in his parable, widely scattering seeds as he goes. He and the twelve are apparently supported by some wealthy women in their entourage who have been healed of various diseases and are now dedicating their lives to the Kingdom.

The phrase "preaching and bringing the good news of the kingdom of God" (v. 1) derives its significance from the "compassion" stories which have preceded it (Luke 7:1–50). The good news is that the Kingdom has come to foreign centurions, widows, prostitutes, lepers, cripples, and the blind and the deaf. Skipping the traditionally righteous, it is now offered to others.

Not all people are able to hear this good news, of course; some are like the hard ground and thorny soil of the parable, and the seed either doesn't take root at all or, if it does, does not come to proper fruition. But Jesus is comforted by the knowledge that some bearers will be like the good soil, in which the seed will reproduce itself a hundred times over. Hearing the good news, they will "hold it fast in an honest and good heart, and bring forth fruit with patience" (v. 15). In a different metaphor, they will trim their lamps and put them on stands in the great entry hall, so that anyone who comes into the house will know immediately that something has happened to their lives.

Be careful then, says Jesus, how you hear; because the person who truly hears all of this will be exceptionally well endowed, while those who don't hear will lose all they have.

At this point Jesus' mother and brothers come to see him. Mark sets this visit in the context of Jesus' conflicts with the scribes and Pharisees, concluding it with Jesus' words that "whoever does the will of God is my brother, and sister, and mother" (Mark 3:35). Matthew follows Mark in both the conflict setting and the wording (Matt. 12:46–50). Luke has apparently altered the saying—though not the meaning—in order to make it tie in with the preceding 20 verses, which are all, in one way or another, about hearing the Word and doing it. Whoever hears the Word he is preaching about the Kingdom for the poor and oppressed, he says, becomes part of his intimate family.

Lord, thank you for the Word of the Kingdom that makes us part of the family of Jesus. Let me continue to hear the Word afresh in every season of my life, that it may never cease to spring up and produce its fruit in my thoughts and actions. In the family's name. Amen.

WEEK 5

Week 5: Sunday

Luke 8:22–39 The Lord of All

Two events, the calming of the sea and the healing of the Gerasene man, are combined in today's reading because Luke probably saw them as having significance in relation to each other. Together, they constitute an excursion in Jesus' ministry. He crosses the sea of Galilee to the country around Gerasa, on the eastern coast of the sea, and then, after healing the Gerasene man, returns to the Galilean side of the sea (v. 40), probably near Capernaum.

The point of it all is that Jesus shows his mastery of both the sea and the demons in the land beyond the sea. In other words, he is master everywhere in the world, not only in Galilee and Judea. Luke's Gospel, we remember, is always careful to exhibit the universal lordship of Christ, and even though the material in this section appears to be derived from Mark (4:35–5:20), he would have welcomed stories that make this point.

The Jews were never a seagoing people, and the sea was to them a symbol of chaos and disorder. In the Book of Genesis, when God created the world, he separated the dry land from the waters; and the Book of Revelation speaks of a new heaven and a new earth in which there is no more sea (Rev. 21:1). To the Jewish mind, the sea with its raging storms represented the last refusal of nature to be tamed.

When Jesus rebuked the wind and waves, producing immediate calm, it was a sign of his absolute mastery of the world. To the question, "Who then is this?" there could be but one answer: He was God's appointed one, with the power of God himself.

The story of the healing on the coasts of Gerasa contains the same kind of cosmic symbolism. The name of the unclean spirit who is devastating the poor man is given as Legion. A legion was a Roman division of six thousand men. Undoubtedly the spirit's name implied that a vast number of demons were residing in the man—far more than afflicted a person in any other biblical story. For Jesus to conquer thousands of demons at once, and on a foreign shore, clearly spelled his universal power.

When we remember Luke's feeling for the "foreign" mission of the church throughout the Book of Acts, we know what special interest he must have had in the witnessing of the cured man to the people of his own region. It would have been important preparation for the later establishment of a Christian colony there.

It is a wonder, Lord, when I think of it, that the power of Jesus not only crossed the Galilean Sea to reach the demon-ridden man of Gerasa, but crossed an ocean to touch my life in America. Teach me to live more constantly in awe of this power and mystery, that I, like the Gerasene, may share my awareness of it with others. For the sake of the Kingdom. Amen.

Week 5: Monday

Luke 8:40–56 A Daughter of the Opposition

There must have been some human drama behind this story that did not get told in the Gospel, for Jairus was the president of the local synagogue, probably in Capernaum, at a time when the religious leaders were beginning to crystallize their opposition to Jesus. Jairus was probably torn between his political position and his personal need for Jesus' power to cure his daughter. Luke heightens the pathos of the story over Mark's account by adding that the girl was his *only* daughter. We can imagine what may have gone on in Jairus's mind before he finally succumbed to his love for his daughter and rushed out to beg Jesus to come and save her. The fact that he fell down before Jesus is an indication of the desperation he felt when he finally sought the Master's help.

The story is interrupted midway, as it is also in Mark's Gospel, by the story of the woman who touched Jesus in the crowd and was healed. Her condition has been identified today as menorrhagia, an unceasing menstrual flow. According to Levitical law, this made her continuously unclean, just as if she had leprosy or some other terrible disease. It was therefore rather daring of her to touch Jesus, for the Law forbade her touching anyone. This may account for her having done so stealthily, and also for Jesus' having discerned her touch among all the flutter of hands and bodies pressing against him in the crowd—her condition was a spiritual offense, in one sense at least, and produced a noticeable effect when brought into contact with the holiness of the Son of God. Again, as in the case of the leper whom Jesus touched in Luke 5:12–13, instead of his being infected by the unclean person, power went out from him to heal the unclean one.

The miraculousness of the healing is underscored by the information that the woman had suffered thus for twelve years "and could not be healed by any one" (v. 43). The best manuscripts available show that Luke omitted the phrase in Mark 5:26 that she "had suffered much under many physicians" who had taken all her money. This is a bit humorous when we remember that Luke himself was probably a physician; perhaps he was protecting the reputation of his fraternity! At any rate, Jesus stressed to the woman when she had come forward publicly that it was her faith in the Kingdom that had done this for her. She was to go in peace—*shalom*—which means gracious fullness.

Meanwhile, word came to Jairus from his house that it was too late, his daughter had died. He repeated the message to Jesus, releasing him from the responsibility of going further. But Jesus challenged the synagogue leader to have as much faith as the poor unclean woman who had worked her way through the crowd to touch him. "Only believe in the arrival of the Kingdom," he said in effect, "and she shall be well." Taking the inner circle of disciples and the girl's parents with him, and brushing aside the scoffers, he entered where the girl was, took her by the hand, and lifted her up as though he had wakened her from a mere nap. We can imagine the great joy that filled the household. "Bring her something to eat," said Jesus. "She's hungry."

Thank you, Lord, for these marvelous vignettes from the life of Jesus. What knowledge of people he had, and what compassion, what power! Let me have faith like this woman's, that, if I will but reach out to touch him, life-giving power will flow into me. Lord, I believe; help thou my unbelief. Amen.

Week 5: Tuesday

Luke 9:1–17 The Roles of the Disciples

This passage serves as a pivot between the first part of Luke's Gospel and the preparation of the disciples to go to Jerusalem and experience the passion there. It is essentially a picture of how the disciples helped in the ministry of Jesus and how he sustained them as a community.

The missionary thrust of verses 1–6 is obviously different from that of Luke 8:1–3, in which Jesus and a large company of followers moved together in an itinerant ministry financed by some wealthy women. Now the disciples are sent out in twos, in order to cover a wider territory, and are given orders to take nothing along for the journey but to move decisively from place to place, depending on the hospitality of friends where they can. When people are unreceptive to their preaching of the Kingdom and performing acts of healing, they are to use the ancient Jewish ritual of shaking Gentile dust from their feet when they reentered the Holy Land, and shake the dust of unbelievers from their sandals. The disciples represent, after all, the new Israel of God.

The hubbub that was raised around the country by this intensive, all-out mission attracted the attention of Herod, who had put John the Baptist to death. Now his uneasy conscience made him wonder if the flurry of new religious fervor caused by Jesus and the disciples was the work of John come back to life. The terse statement that Herod "sought to see him" (v. 9) is a foreshadowing of his meeting with Jesus during the Passover in Jerusalem (Luke 23:8).

The return of the disciples from their barnstorming ministry is the occasion for Jesus to draw aside with them, doubtless to hear reports of their activities and lead them in seeking spiritual refreshment. When the crowds follow them, Jesus continues to preach the Kingdom to them and to heal their infirmities. Then, in the "lonely place," Jesus feeds all of them in a meal obviously symbolic of the Eucharist or Communion. The quality of this messianic banquet is hinted in the fact that "all ate and were satisfied," and that afterwards there were twelve baskets of fragments remaining. The early church could not fail to see the significance of this narrative: Jesus always feeds his people amply in the wilderness places of life!

It is interesting to note that the disciples, who have had such a responsible role in preaching and healing during the recent missionary thrust, now have liturgical responsibilities for the meal. Jesus tells them to give the people something to eat, and orders them to arrange the crowd in orderly groups of "about fifty each." And, finally, it is the disciples who set the food before the people. They are the agents of Christ at the table as well as in the pulpit or by the sickbed.

Lord, the church itself is one of your greatest miracles—the long line of preachers, teachers, healers, pastors, and others who do your will in ministering to the peoples of the world; and the many lay persons who witness and pray and support the work in every way. Thank you for the meal that sustains us all in every place and condition, and for the presence of Christ at the table. Amen.

Week 5: Wednesday

Luke 9:18–36 A New Stage of Understanding

Jesus had been teaching his disciples for many months now, and had even sent them out on their own to preach and heal. It was time to raise their understanding of his mission to a new level. He himself had doubtless begun to see the future more clearly since John's violent death at the hands of Herod.

The conversation began on the reports the disciples brought back from their missionary journeys. Who were the people saying that Jesus was? Accustomed to thinking of the future in terms of the past, they had said that he must surely be John or Elijah or another prophet already dead.

Next, Jesus pressed them to see what their own thinking had become. Peter spoke for the group. They had come to the conclusion that he must be "the Christ of God." Matthew 16:17–19 says that Jesus congratulated Peter on this answer, but Luke merely says that he warned them not to use this title openly, lest it provoke an official reaction before he was ready.

Then, building on what the disciples understood thus far, Jesus proceeded to teach them three things about the near future: (1)

he must suffer and die after being rejected by the religious leadership of Israel; (2) they too must suffer, some of them possibly to the point of death; (3) God would give them victory, symbolized in the resurrection of Jesus himself. Because of these three facts, they must not hesitate to deny themselves and follow him.

There can be little doubt that Luke used the next story about the transfiguration as an illustration to the disciples of what Jesus' resurrection would be like. Alone with him in prayer, they beheld him in strangely altered form. His face was different and his clothing became dazzlingly radiant, as in biblical descriptions of angels. Moreover, he was conversing with Moses and Elijah, the two most popular figures of the Old Testament. They were discussing Jesus' "departure"—actually, in the Greek, his *exodus.* As Moses had led the Israelites out of Egypt to form a new nation, Jesus was about to lead his followers into a new Kingdom. Clearly, God was giving the disciples a picture of the transcendent Christ to verify Jesus' prediction that he would be raised up shortly after being slain.

God himself appeared to the disciples in the form of a cloud, and they heard him speak, saying, "This is my Son, my Chosen; listen to him!" Then the cloud was gone, and so were Moses and Elijah. It was a rare mystical experience, and it would later help them to perceive what was happening after the crucifixion.

Lord, I wonder how many experiences like this I miss because I do not spend my nights and days in prayer as the disciples did. Teach me to apply myself to acts of devotion, that the mysteries of the faith may become more palpable in my own life. Through him who has shown us the way. Amen.

Week 5: Thursday

Luke 9:37–50 A Tinge of Disappointment

The new level of understanding among some of the disciples appears to have been unmatched among others. When Jesus, James, John, and Peter came down from their mountainside experience, a man came to Jesus who had been feeling great frustration with the other disciples. They had been unable to heal his only son of the epileptic convulsions that frequently seized him.

Jesus cured the boy, but not before erupting angrily at the failure of the disciples to trust completely enough in the Kingdom's presence to do the work themselves. His anxiety is clearly the product of the urgency he now felt. The time was short, and they must be able to carry on when he was gone.

How little they understood is emphasized by the argument that soon broke out among them about which of them was the greatest. Jesus had only recently spoken of his own suffering role; now they were contending about their honor and glory. Jesus gave them an object lesson they would never forget. Setting a little child beside him—was it the one he had just cured of epilepsy?—he told them that there was no such traditional status in the Kingdom. Anyone who in his name was kind to a child was great in the eyes of God. God did not reckon worth as the rulers of society did.

The phrase "in my name" evidently spurred John to comment that they had seen a stranger using Jesus' name to perform exorcisms, and that they had forbade this unauthorized use of the Master's name. But Jesus was not concerned about this individual—it was the religious leaders who would never have used his name that really troubled him. His appraisal of the situation was more far-sighted than that of his disciples.

Lord, I too am prone to worry about my greatness. Since I was a child, I have needed recognition and praise. Now I call it "stroking." Forgive me for this smallness, Lord, and lead me into deeper faith and commitment, that my dearest joy may be in serving your little ones, not in receiving the admiration of others. Through Jesus, who died humbly at the hands of those who lived proudly. Amen.

Week 5: Friday

Luke 9:51–10:24 The Fall of Satan

At this point, Luke pictures Jesus as turning toward Jerusalem and the final encounter with the religious leaders there. But the trip is anything but direct, and really seems to be a kind of suspense vehicle within which Luke can impart many of Jesus' teachings.

The trip from Galilee to Jerusalem normally took travelers through Samaria. The Samaritans and Jews had long been at odds, one side claiming that the holy center of life was in Mt. Gerizim and the other that it was in Jerusalem. Jesus' intention of climaxing his ministry in Jerusalem therefore provoked the hostilities of the Samaritans in one village, and this in turn stirred the wrath of James and John. As Elijah had called down fire from heaven (2 Kings 1:9–16), they wanted to do so now, proving the authenticity of their mission for God. But Jesus had rejected such temptations of power early in his ministry (Luke 4:1–13), and now rebuked the disciples for entertaining such a notion.

The commitment to the Kingdom required of followers is revealed in Luke 9:57–62. What was happening was of such intense consequence that there was no room for self-consideration or even for the traditional proprieties of life. The nearest analogy would be that of a military call-up; in a moment of national crisis, there is no time for personal errands.

The urgency of this particular phase of Jesus' mission is also shown in the appointment of the "seventy others"—to distinguish them from the disciples and perhaps from the messengers in Luke 9:51–52. Luke alone records this appointment of the seventy. It is possible that he saw in the symbolism of the number, which according to rabbinic reckoning was the number of the Gentile nations, a forecast of the spread of the gospel into all the world, as he later recorded in the Book of Acts.

The instructions to the seventy were similar to those given the disciples in Luke 9:1–6—they were to go out like persons on an urgent mission, making no advance preparations for their work and carrying nothing that would encumber them as they journeyed. They were not to trouble themselves about orthodox matters of eating and drinking, but to take whatever was offered them, regardless of the proprieties (10:8). Their message was simple: "The Kingdom is near you." This would alert the truly devoted persons but would probably infuriate others. Against the latter, the disciples were to shake the dust off their feet. Their villages would fare poorly when the day of the Lord came in all its terror.

The seventy returned from their mission in great joy—one of Luke's dominant themes—reporting that even the demons had been powerless before them. Jesus' response was to tell them of a vision he had had, of Satan plunging from heaven. Hebrew thought had always pictured Satan as located in heaven, where he acted as a kind of prosecuting lawyer against the godly (cf. Job 1 and Zech. 3:1–5). Jesus in this vision foresaw Satan's complete defeat and expulsion from heaven, so that he could no longer trouble the sons and daughters of men. A great victory was in the offing. This was, and still is, the good news of the Kingdom.

"You have been allowed to participate in unusual power," said Jesus. "But don't rejoice in this. Rejoice rather that your names are written in heaven—that God has foreordained that you would be part of the community he is saving!"

Exultant in the Spirit, Jesus prayed and gave thanks that God had given his Kingdom to simple people like these messengers, and not to the religious masters of the land. They were so fresh, so jubilant, so willing to accept at face value what God was doing! Their lives were not complicated by vain philosophies and the vanities of learning.

In the same mood, he reflected that only God could choose the one who would be his Son. The old men of Israel, with all their knowledge, could not do it. Only God. And, now that God had chosen Jesus, only Jesus truly knew and understood the Father as a Son would—only Jesus and those to whom he imparted the knowledge.

Turning to the disciples, who had seen so much with him, he spoke again of the joy of the Kingdom. "Blessed are the eyes which see what you see!" How many prophets and kings of Israel had wanted to see it, and could not. Old Simeon in the temple had seen it (Luke 2:25–32), and now they were seeing it. There would never be anything in the history of the world more wonderful to see!

Lord, when I shut my eyes and concentrate, I can see it too. The lion lying down with the lamb. The armaments of the world beaten into plowshares. The hungry fed. The poor walking through the city like rulers. The sun shining pleasantly on little children of all races at play together. The strong with their arms around the weak. Satan has fallen, Lord, and is falling, and will one day fall for good. The Kingdom is near us. Let it convert me to the very depths of my being, and let me witness to its presence. Through him you have chosen as Son. Amen.

Week 5: Saturday

Luke 10:25–37 The Real Way to Life

This magnificent story has been told and retold around the world, and has doubtless, in its artless simplicity, converted the attitudes of millions of people about what obeying the Law of God really means.

The lawyer—a scribe—probably asked his question about eternal life more to test Jesus than to get a true answer. He got far more than he bargained for. In Mark's Gospel (12:28–32), it is Jesus himself who summarizes the Law by combining two Old Testament passages (Deut. 6:5 and Lev. 19:18). But Luke recognized this as a combination already made by the rabbis of the time, so that the questioner would have his own ready answer to the question he raised. The dramatic difference between Jesus and the lawyer really lay not between the laws they knew but in how they applied them.

When the lawyer had gotten no more from Jesus than to have his question turned on him, he began to niggle, raising a question this time about his own quotation. "Who is my neighbor?" Again, Jesus wanted to make him answer his own question, but not before posing it in such a manner that he could not escape seeing the inner meaning of the Law.

The dramatis personae of the parable are interesting: a priest and a Levite, both central members of the religious elite of Israel, and a Samaritan, one of the people whom Jews regarded with hostility and prejudice. Luke may have located the story here because of the unfavorable mention of Samaritans a few verses earlier, in Luke 9:51–56. He may also have had in mind the movement of the gospel outward from Judea to Samaria and "the end of the earth" (Acts 1:8).

The man who was beaten was heading away from Jerusalem, toward Jericho. The fact that the priest and Levite both "passed by on the other side" indicates that they were going in the opposite direction, toward Jerusalem, possibly to serve their turns in the temple. As the poor victim was half-dead, there was no way they could be certain without touching him that he had not already died, and to do that would have defiled them according to ceremonial law. They obeyed the Law but missed the whole point of it.

The unorthodox Samaritan, on the other hand, really fulfilled the Law while not even being concerned to obey it. He "had compassion" on the poor man, bound up his wounds, and walked to the nearest inn while the beaten man rode on his beast. There he covered all the man's expenses until he was well enough to travel home. The lawyer could not but admit that the Samaritan was the real neighbor to the man, not the priest and Levite.

When we think about it, we realize that Jesus' entire ministry is summarized in the action of the Samaritan. From the very outset, he chose to have compassion on the poor and oppressed rather than to conform to the hundreds of rules and regulations governing the lives of the scribes and Pharisees.

Lord, I have always admired Samaritans—people who live on the edge of respectable society, yet respond magnanimously to the needs of others. Help me to live more generously and spontaneously myself, that I may better understand the heart of Jesus. In his name. Amen.

WEEK 6

Week 6: Sunday

Luke 10:38–42 The Most Important Thing

The village Jesus is here reported to have entered is doubtless Bethany, which we know from John 11:1 to have been the home of Mary, Martha and Lazarus. In terms of Luke's travel narrative it is highly unlikely that Jesus would have been in Bethany at this point, as it lay barely outside Jerusalem. What Luke has obviously done, then, is to place the story here, omitting the name of Bethany, because he sees a direct relationship between this little narrative and the parable of the Samaritan that has immediately preceded it. This helps us to identify more precisely Luke's own interpretation of the story.

In a way, the story is a gloss or comment on the parable of the Samaritan. Martha, who is anxious to serve Jesus properly, is really a Christian version of the priest and Levite in the parable. That is, she is deeply concerned to fulfill the law of proprieties. Mary, on the other hand, has the soul of the Samaritan. She is more concerned to respond in love than to conform to the rules or duties of the household.

It is surely unfair to brand the Marthas of the world unfavorably because of this passage—in her way, Martha was trying as hard as Mary was to be a compassionate host. Our homes, churches, and other institutions would soon be in pitiable shape if it were not for the selfless service of the caretaking persons.

Jesus' point—and Luke's—was more specific than that; namely, that the *first* obligation of a person is to give responsive love or compassion. When following the rules is put first, the most needful part—the love—is often missed or omitted.

We should be actively involved in society for God—but not before we have taken time to pray and worship. We should work zealously for the church—but not put it before the people who lie outside the membership of the church. We should strive to improve human conditions for the poor, the weak, and the sick—but not without first truly caring for them as persons.

Lord, it is so much easier to feel self-righteous when I am Martha than when I am Mary. When I wait before you in a mood of worship, or when I respond in generous sympathy to the personality of another, I don't even think to value my action. Then I experience true joy. Help me to be more like Mary, without forgetting the value of Martha. Amen.

Week 6: Monday

Luke 11:1–13 The Spirit of Prayer

It is helpful, if we wish to know how Luke felt about this material he was recording on prayer, to remember how prayer is treated throughout the Book of Acts. Never in Acts does any Christian pray for anything for himself. Almost invariably, prayer is for the Kingdom and other persons. It is for the sick, the imprisoned, the unconverted. If the Christian does appear to be at all at the center of his or her praying, it is only to know the will of God for a life of service and self-emptying.

Seen in this light, the present passage is quickly understood to center on the Kingdom. "Thy kingdom come" is the central petition of the model prayer Jesus gives the disciples. All the other phrases derive from this one. As Kingdom people, we ask little for ourselves—only daily bread, not expensive feasts and clothes and property. The emphasis on *daily* bread reminds us of God's provision of manna to the Israelites during their wilderness years; like them, we are a pilgrim people. Our other concerns are to be compassionate and forgiving, as befits those who in the Kingdom are forgiven and accepted, and not to be tested so severely that we abandon the faith. Temptation is not here to be regarded in terms of the nettling little sins of everyday existence, such as the desire for foods we shouldn't eat, the wish for money, or sexual fantasies. It has to do with temptation as Jesus experienced it in the wilderness (Luke 4:1–13), which, if we yield to it, causes us to fall away from our vision of the Kingdom.

Luke's version of the model prayer is considerably briefer than the one in Matthew 6:9–13, and scholars are confident that it is the more original of the two. Matthew's version has merely added liturgical phrases that do not significantly alter the meaning.

Aside from the rhythm of "Our Father who art in heaven," Luke's simpler "Father, hallowed be thy name" is surely preferable as being more in keeping with Jesus' ways and teachings. Professor G. B. Caird says in his commentary: "Any Jew could have prayed, 'Our Father, who art in heaven . . . ,' using the formal and exclusively religious *Abinu*. But when Jesus prayed, he used the word *Abba* with which a child addressed his human father. He transformed the Fatherhood of God from a theological doctrine into an intense and intimate experience; and he taught his disciples to pray with the same family intimacy."

After giving the disciples a form of prayer based on the intimacy between children and their father, Jesus proceeded to speak of the Father's willingness to hear their prayers and respond to them. He will surely be as attentive as a friend who hears us knocking for help in the night, or as earthly fathers who try to give their children the foods they ask for.

Verses 8–10 clearly recommend the importance of praying for our needs, even though God already knows what we require, just as children make requests of their earthly fathers. But verse 13 is equally clear that the gift which Christians are to seek in their praying is the Holy Spirit (Matt. 7:11 reads "good things").

The overall emphasis of the passage, then, is a spiritual one, in keeping with the coming of the Kingdom and the submission of the one praying to the will of the Father. This is borne out again and again in the Book of Acts.

Lord, too much of my praying has not been of a spiritual nature. I have often sought little gifts that would make life more attractive for me, ignoring the fact that the one thing that can change all my life for the better is to submit myself to you and your Kingdom. Then I would know joy indeed, even as the disciples did. Teach me to pray as they prayed, yielding myself to your Holy Spirit. Through Jesus, who was obedient unto death. Amen.

Week 6: Tuesday

Luke 11:14–36 The Sign of Jonah

If we are inclined today to despair over the shallowness of popular Christianity, we need only read this passage to know that things have not changed greatly since Jesus' own time.

First, there were people who doubted the miracles he was performing. Some even attributed his miraculous cures to Beelzebub, "the prince of demons." Jesus dealt forcefully with these persons. Would Satan work against himself, he asked, by casting out his own agents? The people should ask their own magicians and sorcerers, he said; they would tell them how difficult it was to perform true exorcisms! What the people should see was that "the finger of God" (Exod. 8:19) was at work in their midst—then they would realize how near the Kingdom was.

Satan, said Jesus, was like a strong man guarding his citadel. But Jesus had entered the fortress and was plundering the strong man's treasures. Surely the people could see that if they only looked.

Verses 24–26 appear to be a warning to those who had been cleansed of demons. They were like houses which required occupancy. Unless they were filled with the Spirit of God after their exorcisms, they were in danger of being reinvaded, not by one demon, but this time by seven! The same is surely true of people today. The initial excitement of religious attachment is not enough to maintain them—they must be filled with God's Spirit or end in darkness and despair worse than they knew in the beginning.

As Jesus was talking, a woman in the crowd called out an extravagant word of praise roughly equivalent to "Your mother must really be proud of you." But Jesus turned off this word as a bit of mere sentimentality. What is important, he said, is to hear and keep God's word.

Reflecting on those who kept asking for some kind of uncontestable "sign from heaven" (v. 16), Jesus then said that no sign would be given such an evil generation except the sign of Jonah the preacher. Jonah had gone to wicked Nineveh and preached the need for repentance, and Nineveh had repented in sackcloth and ashes. Here was Jesus in a similar role, preaching the coming of the Kingdom. That should be enough, if the people of his day were truly spiritual. But as they were not, the people of Nineveh and the queen of the South would rise in the day of judgment and accuse the Israelites, for they had repented without special signs.

Verses 33–36 are a collection of sayings on the theme of light. Israel had been called to be a light to the nations, but had covered the light she had. The eye, when it is good, causes the whole body to respond to the light; but, when it is bad, it results in the body's being swathed in darkness. The last two verses, which are difficult for all commentators, seem to recommend the results of really being able to see—which is the problem with most of the people in the crowd; they cannot see.

Lord, preserve me from being either too negative or too sentimental about religious faith. Let me watch and listen attentively, that I may discern your Spirit's presence in my life. And grant that I may respond by living in the way of the Kingdom. Through him who showed us the way. Amen.

Week 6: Wednesday

Luke 11:37–12:12 Warnings against Hypocrisy

Here are several sayings of Jesus grouped around the general theme of hypocrisy and truth.

First are a number of scathing remarks about Pharisees and scribes, roughly paralleling those found in Matthew 23. It is unlikely that Jesus ever delivered one long tirade against the Pharisees and scribes, as this arrangement suggests; probably the sayings were grouped thus after having been spoken on several different occasions.

The primary thrust of all the rebukes or "woes" is that the highly orthodox Jews paid much attention to inconsequential matters of the Law while neglecting the important matters—a charge in keeping with other teachings of Jesus, such as the parable of the good Samaritan (Luke 10:25–37), which, we recall, was spoken to a scribe.

They fastidiously scoured the outside of the cup, while completely neglecting the inside, which was more important. They went beyond the expectations of the Law, which said that general agricultural products were to be tithed, and paid a tenth even on their tiny herb gardens which were not worth bothering about; yet they completely ignored the question of justice for the poor and the matter of loving God. They were like unmarked graves, onto which unwary persons might stumble, defiling themselves by coming in contact with the dead. They constructed enormous burdens for the common people to bear, and then refused to help them at all. Having held the key to salvation, they themselves refused to enter the door and, moreover, blocked the way so that others could not go in.

Clearly, they were obstructing the work of the Holy Spirit and would not be forgiven for this (Luke 12:10).

The disciples were warned to beware of the same kind of hypocrisy in their own lives. They would be tempted, when brought before the courts and tribunals, to lie and put on falsehoods in order to save themselves. But Jesus warned them not to join the hypocrites in this manner; they should not fear those who had only the power to hurt their bodies, but the One who had power to punish them by cutting himself off from them forever. The God who cared even for the cheap, insignificant little sparrows could certainly be trusted to care about what happened to them when they suffered for the faith. He would instruct them through his Holy Spirit how to respond in times of crisis when they were hailed before officials of the government.

Lord, the love of your Kingdom converts our natures, so that we no longer higgle over little things that are of small consequence in the lives and affairs of people, but devote our energies to the larger issues, such as feeding the hungry, clothing and sheltering the poor, and healing the sick and tormented of heart. Help me to become an ambassador of your joy, disdaining the cost to myself. Through Jesus, in whom your light shines purely. Amen.

Week 6: Thursday

Luke 12:13–34 A Warning in a Parable

Diogenes is said to have given away all of his possessions except a shard of pottery which he used for drinking. Then he saw a small boy cupping his hands to drink from a stream, and threw away the shard.

Wise people have always realized that possessions can encumber a life until it is barely fit for living. Jesus constantly warned the disciples of the tendency in all of us to enslave ourselves to what we have.

The man who came to him asking for a judgment did so because Mosaic Law was always being interpreted by rabbis. But Jesus refused to accept the problem as a mere civil problem that could be solved by a judge's decision. Instead, he threw the burden back on the man himself, pointing out the importance of caring less about money and property.

The parable of the rich man is still a striking vehicle of truth for people who are careful about providing fiscally for their futures yet absurdly heedless of their spiritual conditions. One wonders what would become of the capitalist way of life and an economy that depends on Detroit and Madison Avenue if many persons took the story as seriously as it deserves.

Considering Jesus' teachings to the disciples about trusting God to provide their daily needs—the model is still that of the Israelites being fed each day in the wilderness—it is no wonder that Luke later pictures the early church as a fellowship of voluntary poverty, sharing from a common treasury. It raises an unavoidable question about our stewardship in the church today. Some churches hold more property than many business corporations in their cities, and have their most serious congregational squabbles over the maintenance of buildings. It is hard to believe that they have really considered the ravens or the lilies.

Lord, there is an incipient greed in me that is hard to kill. I have always felt insecure in the world, and thus want money and property as a hedge against poverty and distress. I am often the very rich man of whom Jesus spoke. Teach me so to apply my heart and thoughts to your Kingdom that I shall cease to be afraid—indeed, that I shall want nothing but the simple everyday things with which you have already supplied us so amply. Through Jesus, who left a great spiritual legacy but no property at all. Amen.

Week 6: Friday

Luke 12:35–48 Living for the Master

The picture here is of genuine enthusiasm in the Master's service. "Girding the loins" was a way of getting ready for action—the long robes of the time were tucked up into the girdle or belt so they would not impede hard work or fast movement. Having the lamps burning also implied readiness, for the wicks must be trimmed and the lamps filled with oil. The disciples were to be like eager servants waiting up in the night for the master's return from a wedding feast. On returning and finding them so devoted, he would be so happy that he would reverse the normal roles, tuck his own robes into his girdle, and serve *them* at the table.

Possibly Luke knew the tradition on which John 13:2–10 is based, about Jesus' taking a towel and serving his disciples. But the symbolism of the feast and waiting is not completely clear. Was Jesus going away for the feast and then returning to the disciples? Is this a picture of the Parousia, or Second Coming? Peter's question in verse 41 is well put, but the answer seems enigmatic. In a way, the lessons apply to both the disciples and the crowds, including the scribes and Pharisees. Doubtless, too, the church saw meaning in them for itself.

It seems probable that Jesus saw the signs of a dark time coming for Israel, and therefore expected an imminent arrival for the great day of the Lord. In the face of this, he warned his followers to be faithfully obeying God's will at all times, so that no sudden cataclysm would take them unawares and result in spiritual disaster. As the special recipients of Christ's teachings, they would be held more accountable than others.

Lord, I tremble to think how accountable I am. You have given me so many insights into the nature of your Kingdom and your desire for my life. Yet I am daily out of harmony with those insights. Help me to be motivated in new ways to fulfill your expectancies for me, that I may rejoice in the coming of my Servant-Master. In his name I pray. Amen.

June 2

Week 6: Saturday

Luke 12:49–13:9 A Fire in the Earth

It is sometimes argued that Jesus and John the Baptist saw the coming of the Kingdom differently; but here is proof that Jesus, like John before him, viewed it as an occasion of extreme stress and suffering for many.

The "baptism" he said he must be baptized with was his death (cf. Mark 10:38). Apparently he saw that as only the beginning of the apocalyptic horror. His very dying would divide households and nations. It was a true word. We know that throughout history, especially in pagan countries, sons' or daughters' becoming Christians has led to expulsion from their families. There are nations throughout Africa and Asia where this still occurs. It is true, moreover, even in our own country, that radical devotion to Christ produces dissension in family groups—most of us prefer to take our faith in moderation!

The signs of the coming of this difficult time, Jesus told the crowds, were all around them. They considered themselves good weather prophets—a small cloud drifting in from the Mediterranean was enough to cause them to forecast rain. They should be more sensitive to the changing of the times, and should be actively trying to appease God, as one would try to appease a person suing him, even on the way to the magistrate's house!

Some people in the crowd raised a question about some Galileans whom Pilate had had killed in Jerusalem—were they terrible sinners, that this happened to them? People are always ready to speculate about retributive justice for those who have suffered. There may also have been some slur implied in referring to the unfortunate Galileans, as Judeans usually regarded them as inferior. "No," replied Jesus; and he shot back with an illustration of tragedy involving Judeans themselves, when a tower collapsed, killing a dozen and a half of them. They were no worse than other Jerusalemites, said Jesus. Pointing to cases like this was useless. What he meant, said Jesus, was that they were *all* in for terrible times unless they repented. God's action was going to destroy an entire nation.

The parable of the fig tree was exactly to the point. The fig tree was often regarded as a symbol of Israel—as her fig trees prospered, she was thought to prosper. Here the tree was unproductive. It took nourishment from the soil of the vineyard without repaying its owner with fruit—precisely as all the prophets had seen Israel doing. The owner instructed his foreman to destroy the tree, but the foreman begged a year's extension for it. He would dig around it, adding manure, to see if that would not cause the tree to produce fruit; if it did not, then it would be cut down and burned for fuel. The ministries of John and Jesus were probably the last chance Israel would have—if they could not turn the people to the way of the Kingdom, then the nation was finished.

Lord, it is so easy for me to be judgmental about Israel and to say the people got exactly what they deserved. What is not easy is to see how true Jesus' words are for me in my moral and spiritual life as well—that I become as complacent and useless as the ancient Jews were. Help me to return to true worship in my life, and to feed others with the fruits of my devotion, lest I too be destroyed by fire. Through him who was baptized in the flames. Amen.

WEEK 7

Week 7: Sunday

Luke 13:10–21 The Sabbath and the Kingdom

How often have we seen people like this poor deformed woman in the crowd and wished we could do something for them! We can imagine their wretchedness, their inconvenience, their pain and discomfort, and our compassion has rushed out to them.

This is how it was when Jesus saw the woman who could not straighten up. He was teaching in the synagogue, not healing. But when he saw her, he instinctively called out to her and healed her. It was an impulsive act of love.

The behavior of the synagogue leader may also have been instinctive. He was accustomed to rules and regulations, and rules and regulations dictated that no work was to be done on the sabbath. This meant the work of doctors as well as the work of farmers, builders, and housewives. Note that his words were directed not to Jesus himself—perhaps he was afraid of this man of power—but to the people. "Not today!" he said. "Not today! There are six days of the week when work may be done. Come back on one of them." He appears to have been a typical slave to routine and bureaucracy.

Jesus knew that the leader spoke thus because of all the others who would complain if the sabbath rules were not kept. Therefore he addressed him in the plural, denouncing the leaders, as he often spoke of the scribes and Pharisees, as hypocrites. "You take care of your animals on the sabbath," he said in effect. "Isn't this poor woman worth more than they are? She is a daughter of Abraham and has been afflicted this way for years. Your animals have been restricted and gone without water a mere twelve hours or so. Isn't it inconsistent to bend the rules for them and not for this woman?"

At this, the people rejoiced—one of Luke's favorite verbs—and his recalling that rejoicing led him to report Jesus' sayings about the Kingdom. Both sayings are about the enormous growth of the Kingdom. It is like the great tree that springs from the tiny mustard seed, making room for the birds of many nations to rest on its branches; and it is like the small lump of leaven in a bowl of batter, that makes the dough swell and regenerate until it is several times its original size. This was truly a cause for joy!

Lord, I have to sympathize with the poor synagogue leader. He was trying to do his job. How our jobs become our masters and make us do things it would not be in our natures to do if we weren't ruled by them! Help me, I pray, to keep my job in perspective, that I may not allow it to diminish my freedom as a person or dehumanize me in my relationship to your world. Through Jesus, who reshaped the roles he had to play and left them resilient and human. Amen.

Week 7: Monday

Luke 13:22–35 The Master and His House

The person who asked Jesus the question in verse 23 was merely being curious. Speculating about when the end would be and how many would be saved had long been the pastime of the idle and pseudoreligious. But Jesus characteristically formed his answer in such a way as to involve the questioner in a life-or-death situation. Brushing aside the question of "how many?" he pointed to the importance of entering the Kingdom when one has the opportunity. Otherwise the person may find himself or herself on the outside and unable to get in through a superficial acquaintance with the Master.

The picture Jesus gave was one of eternal disappointment—of looking in and seeing the great patriarchs of Israel sitting at the heavenly banquet not with them but with outsiders, people from all the other nations. Jesus had already demonstrated this in his ministry by dining with prostitutes and tax collectors—sinners before the Law. But in the Kingdom even the hated Gentiles would go in before the unbelieving Israelites.

It was appropriate that some Pharisees should come "at that very hour" to warn him of Herod's enmity, for such a picture of the Kingdom was the very thing that would provoke the violence of the crucifixion. But Jesus' response was cool and self-governed; he would not be hurried to the climax of his ministry in Jerusalem. When he was ready, he would go, but not before. No earthly sovereign was going to diminish the sovereign authority of the One who was Lord in the Kingdom!

Verses 34–35 are a word of lamentation about the failure of Israel to respond to the good news of the Kingdom. The gathering of Jerusalem's children from the four corners of the world had been a constant dream of Hebrew prophecy (see Isa. 60:4 and Zech. 10:6–10). But the children would not come when he preached the vision of the Kingdom to them. Therefore their nation and temple would lie desolate and forsaken, like ruins caressed by the winds of time.

The last sentence of the passage may be a promise that Jesus would not show up in Jerusalem until the Passover, when the people would shout "Hosanna!" at his entry (Luke 19:37–38). Or it may be a more apocalyptic saying, meaning that the people would not recognize him for who he truly was until the final triumph of the Kingdom. Then they would be like the unfortunate Jews in verses 26–30, who reminded the Master of the house that they had eaten and drunk in his presence and had even heard him teaching in their streets, but had not entered his house in time for the feast.

Lord, these apocalyptic pictures and sayings are frightening to me. They raise deep-seated anxieties about separation and abandonment. They speak of the severity that is the other side of your goodness, and the anguish that is the other side of the joy in your Kingdom. I pray that they will keep alive in me a genuine feeling for the urgency of preaching the gospel to everyone who has not yet heard with inward truth, and for doing *the gospel in my own life.* Amen.

Week 7: Tuesday

Luke 14:1–24 Some Table Talk

"They were watching him." How carefully Jesus was being scrutinized by the scribes and Pharisees, who hoped to entrap him and dispose of him. We could almost conclude that the invitation to dine with this prominent Pharisee was no more than a convenient arrangement to have Jesus where they could observe his every movement.

The man with dropsy was there, either as a guest or as an unbidden onlooker, like the woman who anointed Jesus' feet in Luke 7:36–50. What would the man of great compassion do? He put the burden on the Pharisees—what did they say? They were silent. If they said no, it was not permitted to heal on the sabbath, they would appear inhumane. If they said yes, it was all right, they would be contradicting their laws. So Jesus healed the man and once more (as in Luke 13:11–17) appealed to the humanitarian instincts in them of putting persons ahead of animals.

The next portion of the passage indicates that Jesus was watching his adversaries as closely as they were watching him. What he saw was their jealousy about the seating arrangements—each was anxious to have a place above the others. Always take the low place, Jesus advised them; it is better to be called up than put down.

Jesus also noticed that the host had carefully invited his best friends, kinfolk, and most prominent acquaintances to the meal. That is a mistake, he cautioned; one ought rather to invite the poor, the maimed, the blind, the outcast, who cannot possibly repay the favor. Then God will repay at the time of the resurrection. The Pharisee had been socially sagacious but had completely missed the way of the Kingdom.

It is possible that the early church read in these last verses a lesson to itself, not to strive to have only the finest citizens at the Lord's table; for the Lord himself had announced that the joy of the gospel is for the poor, the blind, and the oppressed (Luke 4:14–30).

And this is precisely the point of the parable in verses 16–24. The parable is given in response to the pious remark of one of the dinner guests. (We have seen a similar stylistic device in Luke 11:27–28, where Jesus reacted to a sentimental saying by a woman in the crowd.) Doubtless the man supposed himself to be included in the heavenly banquet. But Jesus used the occasion to point out again, as he did consistently in all his ministry, that everyone would be surprised when he or she saw the guests at that banquet. They would be the very persons the good Jews were ignoring, while the religious leaders themselves would not taste a morsel!

Lord, the politics of the Kingdom and the politics of this world are often at odds with each other. Help me always to seek the way of the Kingdom in my affairs, that I may rejoice with those who will enjoy the heavenly feast with you. Through Jesus, who watches me as I watch him. Amen.

Luke 14:25–35 Facing the Hard Realities

Despite his continuous conflict with religious leaders wherever he went, Jesus was still extremely popular and had an immense following among the common folk. Yet he was bothered by their lack of comprehension. They did not seem to appreciate the danger of his mission, either to him or to themselves. Therefore he turned on them and attempted to make them face the truth. Discipleship would not be easy, he warned; in fact, it would demand every ounce of loyalty they could summon.

Hating one's father and mother did not mean to the Jewish mind precisely what it means to us. As G. B. Caird has put it, "The semitic mind is comfortable only with extremes—light and darkness, truth and falsehood, love and hate—primary colours with no half-shades of compromise in between. The semitic way of saying 'I prefer this to that' is 'I like this and hate that' (cf. Gen. 29:30–31, Deut. 21:15–17)." What Jesus said, thus, was that their families must take second place, not first; first was for the Kingdom. He himself, we recall, when his mother and brothers came to see him, said, "My mother and my brothers are those who hear the word of God and do it" (Luke 8:21).

Being a disciple, he told them in a daring metaphor, is like bearing your own cross—committing yourself to the gallows, to execution, to death among strangers.

Count the cost, he warned. Even a builder does that before erecting a tower. A king does it before engaging in war. Any reasonable person does it. Therefore disciples should do it too—they ought not to begin a discipleship they cannot complete.

To be a disciple but unable to follow Jesus through times of stress and danger is to lack the real quality of discipleship. It is like being salt that does not have the real power of salt. Such salt is worthless. It is salt in name only, and people throw it out and have done with it.

Lord, these are bracing words. They sting my conscience like nettles, like thousands of needles of fire. What kind of disciple am I? Could I follow to the death, or am I only a disciple of convenience? How selfishly I have heard the gospel. Forgive me, O suffering One, and help me to increase the measure of my devotion, lest I betray you in a moment of forgetfulness or an hour of pressure. Amen.

Week 7: Thursday

Luke 15:1–10 The Kingdom of Joy

Here we come to what is for many the heart of Luke's Gospel. No other Gospel writer has recorded all three of the beautiful parables of this chapter. (Matthew 18:12–14 gives the parable of the lost sheep.) More than any other stories, perhaps, they represent what God was working out through Jesus' ministry.

The setting recorded by Luke is not unlike the one in which Jesus was frequently pictured—teaching and healing the poor, the blind, and the outcast, with the scribes and Pharisees looking on to criticize. This time, as on other occasions, they were complaining about the unsanctified company Jesus kept. They themselves would never have had dealings with such people; they considered contact with them to be defiling and degrading. And Jesus was *eating* with such persons—engaging with them at what Orientals would consider a most intimate level!

It was to answer the criticisms of the religious Jews that Jesus told these rare stories—the parables of the lost sheep, the lost coin, and the lost boy. Each would have been readily understood by those who heard them.

The essential note in each story is the note of joy. The shepherd tracks his errant sheep out in the wilderness where it has wandered, and "lays it on his shoulders, rejoicing." When he comes back, he calls to his friends, saying, "Rejoice with me." Even so, says Jesus, "there will be more joy in heaven" over the sinner who repents. The woman loses a single coin, a silver drachma, worth slightly more than a day's wages in ancient Palestine. Probably it has fallen among the straws or rushes on her earthen floor and is difficult to find in her dark, almost windowless house. She lights a lamp, sifts through the straws, and even sweeps the house, in search of the coin. At last her eye falls on it. She calls her friends together, saying, "Rejoice with me." In the same manner, says Jesus, "there is joy before the angels of God" when a lost sinner is recovered.

The angel who announced the birth of Jesus to the shepherds on the hillside said that he brought them "good news of a great joy" which would come to all the people (Luke 2:10). When Jesus announced the design of his ministry in the synagogue in Nazareth (4:14–30), he identified it with the poor and broken and neglected of the world. Here, in these parables, Luke has drawn these themes together in a climactic fashion. The Kingdom of God is a Kingdom of joy!

Thank you, Lord, for the unmitigated joy of your Kingdom. How wonderful it is to be part of a Kingdom in which everyone has been brought in with rejoicing. Help me to ponder this today, and to realize what it means for my relations with others in the Kingdom. Through Jesus, who led the search for all of us. Amen.

Week 7: Friday

Luke 15:11–32 The Two Lost Sons

There is only one way to the Father, English theologian P. T. Forsyth once wrote—through the far country! Each of us, to appreciate the love and generosity of God, must at some point experience disillusionment with self and the world, come to the point of despair, and then return to the Father in penitence, only to discover that he has been waiting all along with open arms to welcome us.

That is the genius of this story—or part of it, for it is truly one of the most remarkable stories ever told, and certainly one of the best loved. It is rich in human insights—how often two brothers will be so different, one happy and adventurous, the other grudging and insecure. Most of us can readily see ourselves in one or the other. And the picture of God as a father—warm, tolerant, compassionate, forgiving, rejoicing—is surely one of the most compelling we have ever known. It is a perfect story—literary, economical in detail, universal in application, and full of human warmth and understanding.

We do not know why the younger son wanted to go away—perhaps his scrupulous elder brother was getting on his nerves. But he requested and got, according to an ancient tradition of property settlement, his share of the family estate. Off he went to the far country, where he lived like a prince until his money ran out and the country entered a period of famine. At last, in sheer desperation, he found himself in the utterly degrading position of caring for a Gentile master's pigs. Staring at the pods of the carob tree, a kind of nutrient bean fed to cattle and swine, he thought how hungry he was and what good food there was at his father's house, even for the hired servants.

Composing a contrite speech, he arose and returned home. His father, apparently watching the road with a parent's wistful gaze, saw him at a distance, ran out, and embraced and kissed him, despite his obviously broken condition. The boy tried to recite his speech, but was interrupted by the father, who gave bristling commands to the servants to come and care for his son. "The fatted calf" which was ordered slain was a specially grown calf reserved for the most honored guests in the home. It was time to rejoice and celebrate!

That was a story in itself. But Jesus' point in telling it was not served by that episode alone. He wanted the scribes and Pharisees to see themselves in the other episode, when the self-righteous elder brother discovered the party his father was giving for the son who had returned. There was no compassion or joy at all in the elder brother—only a feeling of resentment that this upstart boy, who had earned no place in the home, had come back and was being treated so royally. Perhaps the elder brother would not have minded if the father had taken the boy at his own bargain and hired him as a menial; but to restore him to full sonship and give a feast in his honor was an outrageous affront to his sense of justice. He would have no part of it but complained that *he* had never had such special treatment though he had lived soberly and responsibly these many years.

The point is, the father had the right to decide as he wished in the matter. Near-Eastern fathers were supreme in their households. And he had welcomed his son back. It was too bad the elder son was such a selfish calculating type and could not enter the merriment; he was cutting off his nose, as the phrase goes, to spite his own face. It would have been more fitting, from a human, compassionate standpoint, if he could have joined in the rejoicing with his father and the servants. After all, it was as if a dead man had come back to life again! In the end, the son who had stayed home proved to be more lost to the father's heart than the one who had wandered off.

Lord, there is a streak of the elder brother in me. I too watch what others are receiving, and measure their good fortune by my own. I am grudging when they come off better than I, when I should rejoice for them and enjoy their parties. Help me to feel your presence so strongly in my daily life that I realize there is nothing richer to be had. Then I can truly find joy in everyone's success. Through Jesus, whose stories contain the most remarkable insights. Amen.

Week 7: Saturday

Luke 16:1–13 The Clever Steward

This parable of the steward seems out of place following the three stories of chapter 15. Contextually, it may seem to follow more appropriately after chapter 14, with its warnings about the radical demands on those who would enter the Kingdom. This passage too is directed toward the disciples, though we learn in verse 14 that the Pharisees were listening in.

The point of the parable is the shrewdness with which ordinary business persons act when confronted with a crisis situation, and an exhortation to the disciples to act similarly in the face of their nation's spiritual crisis.

The steward was probably a middle manager who oversaw his employer's tenant farms. When word of his improper handling of affairs reached the employer, the employer gave him notice of dismissal. Quickly taking stock of himself at his present stage of life, the steward decided he was too old to work in the fields and too proud to beg in the streets. So he decided to do something to cushion his fall. Before his employment fully expired, he went to his employer's tenants. The rent on one tenant's property had been fixed at a hundred measures of olive oil, part of which probably went to the steward himself. Using his authority to fix rents, the steward made a good friend of the man by reducing the rent by half. Going to another tenant, he followed the same tactic. Probably there were still others not mentioned for the sake of the parable's economy. The steward was cleverly making friends who would take him in when his employment terminated.

Some commentators believe the master of verse 8 to be Jesus himself, speaking well of the steward. This seems unlikely, as we have no other parable in which the Gospel writer switches to third-person description in this manner to have Jesus comment on his story. It is more likely, given the second half of the verse, that the master here is the same one referred to in verses 3 and 5, namely, the steward's employer. As a businessman, he might have regretted the steward's lack of trustworthiness, yet he could not but admire his ingenuity and praise him for it. The second half of the verse, then, is Jesus' comment: these businessmen are often wiser than the followers of God!

It is possible that the original parable ended here, with verse 8, and that the additional sayings were gathered to it because Luke or some earlier author saw a connection between them and the parable. The phrase "unrighteous mammon" was often used by rabbis to denote money that was legally obtained but not spiritually approved. Interest money or usury often fell under this category. The Law permitted people to take interest on money or property loaned to the poor, even though it was understood that God might not really approve such unmerciful behavior. Verse 9 draws the conclusion from the parable that, like the steward, we should take every opportunity to create friendships with our money or profits, thus earning an eternal merit. Verses 10–12 then suggest that if we do not behave in this manner with the world's goods, God can surely not entrust to us the greater spiritual riches of his Kingdom. We should remember that it is Luke, in Acts 2:44–45, who records that the early Christians sold all their possessions and held what little wealth they had in common, and then, in Acts 5:1–11, tells the story of Ananias and Sapphira, who lost their lives for dealing selfishly and untruthfully with the Christian community.

The final verse, verse 13, links the whole business again to the call to radical commitment in chapter 14, because it restates the importance of wholehearted allegiance. If we love God, we will use our money for spiritual purposes. But, if we love money, we cannot use God to further our business situations. He will not be a party to our selfish designs.

Lord, this is an ingenious story—so daring and imaginative. It invades the world of profit and loss to illustrate for us the great importance of living creatively for your Kingdom. Teach me to think prudently, as this steward did, and to use all my resources and energy in behalf of those who matter to you. Through Jesus, who served you completely. Amen.

WEEK 8

Week 8: Sunday

Luke 16:14–31 The Evidence of the Heart

To read this passage correctly, we must see it in the context of the preceding verses, the story of the clever steward (Luke 16: 1–8), which Luke says was spoken to the disciples. The Pharisees, listening in, scoffed at Jesus for teaching thus. Luke points out that they loved money, and the records do indicate that they often used their superior knowledge of the Law to financial advantage, thereby establishing themselves as the upper class in Israel.

Jesus' response to the Pharisees was pointed: They might know how to justify themselves legally before men, but God would not be fooled, for he knew what was in their hearts. Even though the Kingdom was being preached and those who entered it did so "violently" (that is, by repentance and conversion, which constituted a radical personal readjustment), the Law was not really altered by it. Every part of it would stand despite all the scribes' and Pharisees' clever attempts to manipulate it to their advantage. Even though they had figured out ways to divorce their wives legally, they would find themselves guilty of adultery.

To show how God judges by the heart, Jesus then told the parable of the rich man and Lazarus. Among the Pharisees, the rich man would have been highly regarded. He was enormously wealthy, as indicated by the purple and fine linen clothes and the daily feasts. And there is absolutely no indication that he was not a highly respectable citizen. But God knew him differently, for God saw how he neglected the care of the poor man who lay in sickness and need at his gate. So when the rich man died, he found himself in utter destitution. Now it was the poor man who was well off and the rich man who was crying for mercy—mercy he had never shown the beggar at his gate.

For the first time we are shown some evidence that the man can think of someone other than himself. He worries about his five brothers, who apparently are also wealthy and oblivious of the needs of the poor. Unless they are warned, they too will come to a similar fate. Curiously, the man asks that Lazarus go to warn his brothers—even though his presence at the rich man's gate had not been sufficient warning for him! But Abraham says no. The Scriptures should be enough warning for anybody—they repeatedly describe what God expects of his people.

The message should have been a powerful one to the Pharisees, who were always asking for "signs." They would not behave differently, Jesus said, even if someone returned from the dead to warn them. Their hearts were not right with God. They simply twisted the Scriptures to suit their purposes, and they must answer for it.

•

Lord, how could it be any clearer? Your will for me is to use all that I have for your little ones. No law or rationalization can protect my selfish interest from your condemnation. When I withhold anything, I keep it from Christ. Have mercy on me, O Lord, and teach me to give myself completely. Amen.

Luke 17:1–10 A Miscellany of Sayings

Here Luke recorded an assortment of Jesus' sayings that bear on discipleship—perhaps because the previous chapter dealt partly with that subject.

The first saying (vv. 1–2) is about causing "little ones" to sin. Matthew 18:6–7 and Mark 9:42 both clearly show that "little ones" to them meant disciples, so that is the probable meaning here. It is a tender appellation, much in keeping with the picture of the lost sheep, lost coin, and lost boy of chapter 15. As to what kind of temptations would lead a little one to sin, we can only conjecture. Perhaps in line with the meaning of temptation in the narrative of Jesus' wilderness experience (Luke 4:1–13) and the use of the word in the model prayer (Luke 11:4), it has to do with forsaking the Kingdom of God, falling away from the faith. Woe to the man or woman who causes any follower to shrink back from the life of the Kingdom!

The second saying, verses 3–4, is about forgiving a brother or sister in Christ. Seven times a day, like Matthew's "seventy times seven" (18:22), is a figure of speech implying endless patience and forbearance, qualities which are expected of disciples who have themselves been forgiven enormous debts (cf. Luke 7:40–47).

The third saying, verses 5–6, regards the power of faith. The reason for Jesus' reference to the sycamore tree may be its reputation for an extremely large and intricate root system, making it especially difficult to dislodge.

The fourth saying, verses 7–10, is not commonly known or preached upon today, but it is an extremely rich one for contemplation. It may originally have been spoken for the Pharisees, though it applies equally well to disciples of that or any age. Its point is that as servants of God we should never expect special attention for duties we have performed. Instead, we should maintain attitudes of humility, knowing that no works can ever make us worthy of the grace and presence of our Lord.

O God, the irony of this scripture is that, unworthy as I am, you have *prepared a table for me and invited me to eat and drink. I am overwhelmed by your grace and what the banquet has cost you. I only hope that the dedication of my life will reveal in a small way how enormously grateful I am. Through your Son Jesus, who provides the bread and the wine.* Amen.

Week 8: Tuesday

Luke 17:11–19 The Grateful Foreigner

Gratitude has always been closely allied to realizing the presence of God. People who are negative and ungrateful can be counted upon to be insensitive to the mystery on which their lives really border. If they only knew—only realized—how near God is to them, it would make all the difference in the world for them!

This little story puts the rate of thoughtful, grateful persons at one in ten. There were ten lepers—ten outcasts obviously of different nationalities, brought together by their common affliction. That is a lesson in itself, if we think about it. Being a leper was hard. It wasn't only the disease that was bad—the social penalty for having it was an additional hardship. Lepers had to maintain a distance between themselves and all other persons, even the members of their families. Hence, to have leprosy was to be cut off from all normal relationships in life. It was only as those who suffered from the disease associated with others in the same fix that they maintained any consistent human contact.

We note that these ten lepers "stood at a distance" when they called on Jesus for help. It must have been a pathetic sight, and we have seen throughout the Gospel of Luke how compassionate Jesus was. He had only to see them to wish to help them. "Go and show yourselves to the priests," he told them. This was in keeping with Leviticus 13:9–17, which gave explicit instructions for those having leprosy and wishing a clean bill of health. In

Luke 5:12–14, Jesus healed a leper and then sent him to the priest. Here, the lepers were ordered to go to the priest in the faith that they would be whole. As they were on their way—the Jews probably to Jerusalem and the Samaritan to Mt. Gerizim—the leprosy left them.

One of the ten, the Samaritan, when he found himself whole again, returned to thank Jesus. He was "praising God with a loud voice," says Luke. Jesus spoke words tinged with irony when he saw the man return. "Where are the others?" he asked. "Were there not ten? Where are the Jews? Is this Samaritan the only one who is grateful for what has happened?" (v. 18, P).

The implication is probably wider than the healing incident and the story of gratitude versus ingratitude. To Luke, the narrative was probably a harbinger of the times recorded in Acts, when the recognition of the Kingdom would often fare better among the Samaritans and Gentiles than in Israel itself.

Lord, teach me to seek your face each morning and evening, that I may daily live in sensitivity to the countless gifts surrounding me—gifts I perceive only when I am aware of your presence in my life. Through Jesus, who always lived this way. Amen.

Week 8: Wednesday

Luke 17:20–18:8 The Great Day at the End

These sayings are all related to the End of all things, which was a subject of much speculation among the ancient Jews. They remind us that the coming of the Kingdom had a negative side for those who would be unfavorably judged by its arrival; while it meant joy and fullness to the poor, blind, sick, and oppressed, it meant sudden terror and destruction to others.

First the Pharisees asked Jesus when the Kingdom was coming. They probably wanted to know what would be the signs of the

End. To them, Jesus replied that the Kingdom was already among them, in their very midst. They were seeing the works of the Kingdom wherever Jesus went. They should be repenting and entering the Kingdom.

Then Jesus addressed the disciples about the End. What he had to say to them was not really inconsistent with what he told the Pharisees—it was merely said from a different perspective. They knew the Kingdom was among them; but he talked to them about how it would be in the final hours of the present world order.

They should not be anxious about the coming of the End, thinking that every report of a local catastrophe was evidence of the End. If the End should come, they would know it; the Son of man will appear everywhere, like lightning flashing from horizon to horizon. Before that, he must suffer and die. But, when the day comes for him to be revealed, everything will happen suddenly, as the floods came when Noah entered the ark and Sodom was destroyed by fire when Lot left it.

There will be no time, in the End, to make any preparation or retrieve anything left behind. The person on the housetop cannot run down the side stairs and enter the house for his belongings, or the one in the field return to the head of the row to fetch the coat he left there (cf. Mark 13:16).

As in times of natural calamity, some persons will appear to be absurdly singled out for destruction while others are untouched. Two people will be asleep in the same bed (there is no warrant in the Greek for the KJV's "two *men* in one bed"), and one will be taken while the other is not. Two women will be standing side by side at the same grist mill, gossiping as they work, and one will be swept away while the other remains. Such a picture intensifies the sense of divine power involved—human intervention will be futile when the End occurs.

The disciples wanted to know where the End will come. The answer is somber—the vultures will gather where the corpse lies. Israel is a charnel house, full of death and putrefaction. The vultures have an uncanny way of finding their prey.

Finally, Jesus told a parable encouraging the disciples to pray constantly for the End to come. As the judge eventually gave in to the persistent woman, so God would one day accede to their prayers. Revelation 5:6–14, which pictures the day of "the Lamb who was slain" and is now worthy to receive power and glory, speaks of the golden bowls of incense which the angels take from the altar of God and which are "the prayers of the saints." The praying of God's people will hasten the day when everything will be reordered and renewed.

Lord, it will surely help to shape my daily existence if I pray sincerely for the day of the Lamb to come. My very being will strain toward that great event. Grant therefore that these images may remain vivid in my mind, both consciously and unconsciously, and that I may truly pray, "Thy Kingdom come." In the name of the Lamb himself. Amen.

Week 8: Thursday

Luke 18:9–14 The Braggart and the Beggar

The essence of this poignant little story derives from the Pharisee's failure to realize that he stood in the presence of God. Had he known that—had he felt even an inkling of it—it would surely have caused him to fall prostrate upon the ground, tearing his garments and bewailing his unworthiness as the humble tax collector did. But his religion itself blinded him to the possibility of the Lord's *shekinah* or unspeakable presence. He was so busy congratulating himself for fulfilling all the rules for piety—he fasted even when it was not required and paid tithes even on the smaller things in his possession though the Law did not require it—that he had no real thought for the awesome activity in which he was engaged, speaking to the Almighty God of Hosts. Ironically, he saw the tax collector prostrating himself and suffering the remorse of sin, and instead of being reminded of his own need of forgiveness, he idly added to his prayers that he was grateful not to be like that poor fellow over there.

How aptly this story fitted many of the Pharisees Jesus encountered in his ministry—they too counted their days of fasting and were scrupulous in their tithing, but missed the real secret of spirituality, which is to dwell sensitively in the presence of the living God. It was no wonder that Jesus said the Kingdom would be taken from them and given to prostitutes and tax collectors. At least the latter would have some feeling for the majesty of God when they came before him!

Lord, save me from pretentiousness and self-deception when I pray. Let the sublime mystery of your presence radically humble my spirit, bringing me into a new alignment with the world around me. For you are the living God, and greatly to be feared. Amen.

Week 8: Friday

Luke 18:15–30 The Sadness of a Ruler

There is an obvious contrast in this passage between the carefree innocence of the children and the sad, responsible nature of the ruler. Luke, like Mark, has set them side by side in order to point up this difference. The poor and oppressed are able to hear the good news of the Kingdom because they have nothing to lose and everything to gain. They are like the children. But there are others, like this ruler, who find it difficult to enter the Kingdom because it will mean surrendering their trust in earthly possessions. Thus the good news that means joy to some means sadness to others.

The ruler was probably a leader of a synagogue, not a ruler in the sense of being a king or potentate. Matthew includes the information that he was young (Matt. 19:20). He was apparently a very impressive young man, possibly a Pharisee who had kept the Law fastidiously, yet had a lot of money.

The tip-off to his attitude, in Luke's version, is the way he addresses Jesus as "good." Jesus does not actually try to deny his own personal goodness but to relocate the young man's sense of values. Beside God, there is no goodness—not even in the serious, self-disciplined ruler. The Law is good to follow as a moral guide to life, but it is not God and does not impart eternal life.

Jesus' demand that the man sell all his possessions—perhaps some farms, some town property, and many herds of sheep or camels—and give the money to the poor is designed to jar his dependency from his earthly power and respectability so that he may instead begin to place it on God. It is the fact that this dependency on worldly values has sunk such deep roots in him over the years that leads to his sadness. Perhaps he realizes the greater good he is missing, but cannot shake his need for power and property.

We do not know Peter's motivation for reminding Jesus that he and his friends had left all they had to follow Jesus. Perhaps it was a bit of self-congratulation. Or perhaps he saw Jesus look wistfully after the young man as the man went away, and wanted to speak a consoling word, such as, "Don't feel too bad, Master. Not everyone responds that way. Look at us—we left everything to come with you." And out of his reverie Jesus replies, in effect, "You're right—and everyone who has left anything will have more than he left, both now and in the age to come, when the Son of man is revealed."

Lord, I have more than I need to live. Grant that I may feel you so intimately present to me that I shall not be dependent on what I have, but may become more generous with it, sharing with those who have less. In Jesus' name. Amen.

Week 8: Saturday

Luke 18:31–43 What a Blind Man Sees

Luke now concludes the long section of teachings, begun in 9:51, during which Jesus and the disciples were supposed to be moving constantly toward Jerusalem. Before the section began, Peter had confessed that Jesus was "the Christ of God" (Luke 9:20), and Jesus had taken Peter, James, and John into the mountain with him, where they had witnessed a prefiguring of his resurrection (Luke 9:28–36). Jesus now reminds the twelve again that he must suffer and die, but they are not able to understand any of what he is talking about.

It is ironic, then, that the person who greets him as Son of David while he passes through Jericho is a blind man. The disciples, who have been with Jesus for months, and whose eyes are perfectly good, cannot "see" what Jesus tries to tell them. But the blind man "sees" perfectly well who Jesus is, and will not be silenced by those who try to stifle his outcry.

This is the only time in the Gospel when this messianic title is used. It is as if God had revealed the secret of the messiahship to a man who could not behold a sunset or look into the faces of people passing him in the road. And how appropriate it was that he should be the one to announce the Savior's approach to the Holy City, for Jesus had said at the beginning of his ministry that the coming of the Kingdom meant restoration of sight to the blind (Luke 4:18).

Jesus restored the man's vision. But he would never again see with more genuine perception than he had shown in recognizing the One who was drawing near to Jerusalem.

Lord, many things pass within the angles of my vision. Yet I fear that I do not see with enough true perception. Sight does not often enough become insight. Help me to listen better and watch more intently in your presence, that I may learn to see as this blind man did. Through Jesus, who is able to restore sight to the sightless. Amen.

WEEK 9

Week 9: Sunday

Luke 19:1–10 An Outstanding Sinner

This is the only time in the New Testament we encounter the title of "chief tax collector." Apparently Zacchaeus was in charge of all collections for the Roman government in the city of Jericho. This meant that he was free to keep part of all the money collected by the other tax officials in the city and perhaps in the entire region, and it accounts for the fact that he was very rich.

It also means that Zacchaeus was probably doubly despised by the orthodox Jews in the area. Any tax collector was considered unclean and sinful because it was necessary for him to enter the "unclean" houses of Gentiles and common people of the land, where strict food ceremonials were not practiced, and because he dealt in Roman coinage bearing the image of Caesar. But a *chief* tax collector, by the same token, must have been regarded almost as a chief of sinners!

Luke may have seen added significance, then, in placing this story where he did, as Jesus was right on the verge of entering Jerusalem for his passion. Certainly it emphasizes once more the point that has been made all along in the Gospel, that the Kingdom of God is coming to those who were not expected to have any part in it. This is the special meaning of verses 9–10, which emphasize that Zacchaeus, even though an outcast from orthodox Judaism, is nevertheless a son and heir of Abraham, and a participant in the promise that was made to Abraham.

The human drama of the story has always made it a favorite with preachers and hearers alike. Here was a wealthy publican, his curiosity piqued by the large crowds and the rumors about Jesus, climbing a tree in order to see the Master. And the Master stopped the procession right under that very tree, bade Zacchaeus to come down, and went home with him. Zacchaeus, says Luke, was joyful. This doubtless infuriated the religious leaders of the town, and fitted perfectly with other stories they had heard about Jesus' carelessness regarding the rules of piety.

But Zacchaeus himself was so moved by his visit with the Master that his entire economic behavior was drastically changed. He went far beyond the law in Leviticus 6:5, which required that anything falsely taken from another be restored in full plus one-fifth as penalty—he would make restitution at the rate of 400 percent! Besides that, he would immediately give half of his wealth to the poor.

This was surely a great object lesson for any wealthy persons who became Christians in the early centuries—they could see that sharing with the poor and living in honest simplicity were part of the ethics of the Kingdom. And the story contrasts markedly with the narrative about the wealthy young synagogue ruler in Luke 18:18–25, who could not readjust his priorities enough to give to the poor and enter the Kingdom.

Lord, I understand Zacchaeus's great joy at receiving Jesus in his home. Help me to receive him daily, that my spirit too may be utterly converted to charity. For his name's sake. Amen.

Week 9: Monday

Luke 19:11–28 A Double Parable

This version of the parable of the talents is somewhat more complicated than Matthew's (25:14–30) because it combines the theme of the servants' trustworthiness with the punishment of the citizens who opposed the king's rule. In Matthew, the parable was obviously directed against the Pharisees, who had received various gifts in trust from God but had unimaginatively buried them in the ground to protect them from loss or injury in the marketplace; the Kingdom would be taken from them and given to others.

But Luke has a different application in mind, as he indicates in verse 11. He wishes to use the parable as a comment both on Jesus' absence and on the expectation of many disciples that the Kingdom would come immediately. And the story cuts two ways—to those who are appointed servants of the Lord and to those who have strongly opposed his rule all along.

As for the servants, it is probable that Luke sees these as representing the servants of Jesus—possibly even the disciples themselves—and not the Pharisees. While Jesus is away (clearly he is the nobleman) receiving his kingship, they are to act wisely and resourcefully with the small sums of money he gives them. (In Matthew the sums were much greater; here they are clearly to be used as a test.) When he does return as a king, the Lord will call them to account and reward the faithful ones with the rulership of cities, while depriving the unfaithful ones of everything.

The unruly citizens in this parable are probably the scribes and Pharisees and any other persons who for any reason have refused the Kingdom. There was a historical precedent which may have formed the basis for this part of the parable. When Herod the Great died in 4 B.C., his son Archelaus went to Rome to ask Augustus Caesar to appoint him King of Judea, and a deputation of fifty Jewish citizens followed him to oppose the appointment. Augustus did appoint Archelaus, and, though history is silent about whether he exercised reprisals against his opponents, it is almost unthinkable that he did not. The harshness of verse 27 would suggest that he did, if the parable owed anything to the story of Archelaus, because it does not seem characteristic of the Jesus of Luke's Gospel. At any rate, the story promises an unhappy end for those who stand in the way of Jesus' coming rulership.

Lord, is it ever possible that I stand in the way of your Kingdom? I fear it, not out of any intentional opposition, but because I am not as thoroughly committed to your will as I ought to be. Forgive me, and help me to be converted to your way, that the Kingdom may come more swiftly. In Jesus' name. Amen.

Week 9: Tuesday

Luke 19:29–44 A Time of Joy and Sadness

To appreciate fully Jesus' use of the donkey or ass's foal here, we must remember the stress ancient societies placed on dramatic action. Prophets often used symbolic, nonverbal actions to signify important moments or "messages." For months now, Jesus had been on his way toward Jerusalem, warning his disciples repeatedly that the final conflict with the authorities would occur there. His concern to dramatize his entrance, therefore, was most appropriate. He was entering the city as a king on a peaceful mission, even though certain parties would bitterly oppose him, just as the citizens refused the reign of the newly appointed king in the parable of Luke 19:11–27.

The approach to the city drew great shouts of joy and acclamation from the multitude of Jesus' followers. Their praise was "for all the mighty works that they had seen" (v. 37). The words they used were from Psalm 118:26—words probably spoken originally as a priestly blessing on a king coming to the temple after great victory in the field. Luke is therefore correct in the spirit, if not the letter, when he inserts the word "King" in verse 38, as neither

Mark (11:1–10) nor Matthew (21:1–9) does. Jesus had won a victory in the field and had come to Jerusalem for the final contest.

The disciples' enthusiasm could not be restrained. As we deduce from Luke 19:11, many of them apparently thought the Kingdom was about to come in all its glory. Typically, the Pharisees did not see things the same way. Either they considered the disciples' words blasphemous or they were afraid the Romans would regard them as seditious and take reprisals against all the Jews; so they demanded that Jesus silence the elated crowd. But Jesus knew how natural the disciples' excitement was. They had indeed seen vast evidence of the Kingdom's arrival, and they expected the arrival to be consummated soon. If they were muzzled, said Jesus, nature itself would have to cry out. The time was at that point of fullness.

Still, Jesus himself did not quite share the crowd's elation. He understood better than they what was transpiring. Therefore, staring at the city either from atop the Mount of Olives, looking straight across at the walls, or from the valley, looking up at the imposing profile rising above him, Jesus began to weep over the people's fate. They had refused the Kingdom. There was only one course open to them—they would be overrun by the Roman army during a time of rebellion. The Romans would push dirt ramparts up to the great walls, rush in over them, slay the inhabitants of the city, and then systematically lay the city in ruins—all because the people did not recognize the time of their "visitation."

Lord, how many times have I missed a visitation in my own life because I did not stop to watch for you and recognize your approach? How many times have I failed to see you in a beggar, a mourner, or a child? How often have I been preoccupied with self and selfish values when you bade me leave them all to follow you? I am sad too, Lord, the way Jesus was sad over the city. I really want to know you when you come. Grant that I may be more sensitive to your comings and goings. Through him who always knew. Amen.

Week 9: Wednesday

Luke 19:45–20:8 Intensifying the Conflict

The Gospel of Mark locates the cleansing of the temple on the day *following* Jesus' entry into Jerusalem (11:12–17). Matthew (21:12–13) and Luke both place it together with the entry, indicating that they regarded it as a significant overture to the week of conflict with the priests, scribes, and Pharisees that led finally to the crucifixion. It was an act of authority that clearly provoked the wrath of the religious leaders of the nation.

It is ironic, when we think about it. Throughout his ministry, Jesus was dogged by pietistic scribes and Pharisees who complained that Jesus and his disciples were not strict enough in their observance of religious rules and practices. Now, in this passage, Jesus is seen doing exactly the same to them. He reminds them that Isaiah 56:7 said the Lord's house was to be a place of prayer and chides them for having turned it into a thieves' warren by overcharging the pilgrims who come to Jerusalem.

Luke curiously abridges the account of the cleansing in Mark, omitting the fact that Jesus drove out those who were buying as well as those who were selling. He also neglects to draw the direct line Mark drew between the purging of the temple and the severe displeasure this provoked among the priests and scribes.

But the fact of the priests' and scribes' displeasure is there, and that is the important thing. They were seeking ways to destroy this strong, resourceful enemy of their system, just as the devotees of any system will try to crush the opponents of that system. The one thing blocking their way was the people, for Jesus was an exceedingly popular figure. They had to be careful, and so proceeded during the next several days to try to entrap him with clever questions.

One of these questions concerned his authority to do the works he did. They probably expected Jesus to assert that he was the Messiah sent from God. If he did, they would run to the Roman governor and charge him with sedition, for Messiah-fever always ran high in Passover season and the Romans were especially wary then of any possible uprising in the populace.

But Jesus was cagey. He returned a question for a question. Whence was *John's* authority—his baptism—from heaven or from human sources? The questioners were stupefied. If they said "from heaven," it would validate Jesus' own ministry. If they said "from men," then the people would react angrily, because they held John in great esteem. Lacking the moral courage to grasp either horn of this well-posed dilemma, they simply refrained from answering.

"If you won't give me an answer," said Jesus in effect, "then you won't have one from me."

Lord, why is it we resent anybody who does not fit into our systems? What compels us to oppose, harass, and even destroy him or her? I admit it is that way with me too. Help me to live so in your presence that I shall be more compassionate and tolerant. Through Jesus, who bids me enter the Kingdom. Amen.

Week 9: Thursday

Luke 20:9–18 The Coming of the Son and Heir

As citizens of occupied territory, Palestinians were doubtless very familiar with the absentee landlord practice. Many farms and vineyards in their country were owned by people who lived in Asia Minor, or even in Rome, and were worked by local tenants who did pretty much as they liked. We can imagine the consternation some of these tenants felt from time to time when a representative from the owner appeared and demanded an accounting of the property's management. Sometimes representatives were assaulted and killed just as this parable describes.

The story was very apt, as all Jesus' parables were, for the hearers could readily see the scene Jesus was setting. The hook in it, of course, was the line about the owner's sending his son to the tenants, who summarily rejected him, as they had the earlier emissaries, and killed him. It was true in real life that if the owners of property died or were killed, the tenants living on the property had first legal claim on it. Jesus was accusing the religious establishment of Israel of wanting to be rid of him in order that there would be no impediment to their assuming complete proprietary rights to their nation's life and spirit. But God was not some powerless owner residing at an impossible distance from Israel; he would come and destroy the tenants, and give the vineyard to other tenants.

The expression "God forbid!" appears only in Luke and not in the other Gospels. It is probably a reaction which interprets Jesus' prophecy as a prediction that Jerusalem itself would be destroyed.

The quotation about the rejected stone in verse 17 is from Psalm 118:22–23, and was apparently a favorite text among early Christians, who associated it with the Resurrection. Luke quotes it again in Acts 4:11, in the sermon of Peter before the high priests, scribes, and elders. The last verse of our passage is clear enough: anyone (such as the wicked tenants) who falls afoul of the One who is the cornerstone is found to be broken by the encounter!

Interestingly, Mark's account of the parable (12:1–12) has the son's death occurring inside the vineyard. But both Matthew (21:33–46) and Luke have altered the wording to have the death take place outside. We assume that this was to make the parable conform to the fact that Jesus was crucified outside the walls of the city (Heb. 13:12).

Lord, for me the terrible thing about this story is the realization that my life is your vineyard too, and that I have often turned away your servants and your beloved Son from taking control of it. Forgive me for my rudeness and possessiveness, and help me in the future gladly to surrender whatever you wish from your vineyard. For it is rightfully yours and your Son's. Amen.

Luke 20:19–26 The Things That Belong to God

Jesus' parable of the vineyard (Luke 20:1–18) could not but have reminded his Jewish audience of Isaiah's comparison of Israel to a vineyard (5:1–7), so there was no doubt in the minds of the religious leaders that he had indeed "told this parable against them." They would have liked to seize him immediately and silence him for good, but were still afraid of his popular following. If the people created a tumult, it might provoke the Romans, who would then fulfill Jesus' prophecies about the destruction of the city. So it was necessary for the leaders to bide their time and carefully gather evidence to present to Pilate, the Roman governor, when they finally arrested Jesus and took him before the authorities.

Verses 21–22 are an example of their clever data-gathering. The question they asked turned on the annual poll tax which Jewish citizens must pay to the Roman government, and pay in silver denarii bearing Caesar's image. If Jesus gave a popular answer, that it was morally wrong for worshipers of God to handle money extolling the divinity of Caesar and to pay for the support of a heathen government, then his enemies could instantly bring him before Pilate on the charge of sedition. If, on the other hand, he approved the payment of the tax, it would cause a great rift among his followers and weaken his popular support. Either way, he must lose. But it is evident from the way the question was posed ("We know that you . . . truly teach the way of God") that the questioners really wanted him to take the popular antigovernment stand, giving them the political ammunition they needed.

Coolly and shrewdly Jesus returned an answer that acceded to neither of their desires (vv. 24–25,P). "Whose image and inscription are on the coin?" he asked. "Caesar's," they answered. "Then it is Caesar's," he said. "Give it to him." Technically, it *was* Caesar's—all coinage issued by an emperor remained legally his, although used by his subjects. But there was another part of the answer: "Give what belongs to God to him as well."

At a stroke, Jesus had not only ingeniously eluded the trap set for him, but had reaffirmed the nature of the Kingdom he was preaching. It was not to be a Kingdom in rivalry with earthly kingdoms, commandeering their thrones and taking possession of their coinage. Jesus had settled that when he rejected the temptation to have power and glory from all the nations of the world (Luke 4:5–8). His was a Kingdom of another dimension, to be won through suffering and death. It is no wonder that his enemies marveled at his answer and became silent.

Lord, Caesar's kingdom bothers me a lot. I spend much of my energy worrying about taxes and reports and making ends meet. I think that if I spent more time contemplating your Kingdom I would have more energy for dealing with Caesar, as Jesus obviously did. I am going to try to do that, with your help. Amen.

Week 9: Saturday

Luke 20:27–44 The Lord of the Living

I once heard a rabbi shock a group of Christian ministers by announcing to them that Jesus took many of his teachings from the Pharisees. When pressed for an explanation, he pointed out that the Pharisees were the liberal thinkers of their day, as opposed to the far more conservative Sadducees, and that Jesus agreed with their teachings on such important matters as the resurrection of the dead and the existence of angels and demons.

The rabbi was right, at least up to a point. The Pharisees, like Jesus, did hold certain theological beliefs which developed late in the history of Judaism and did not find expression in the Torah or Law of Israel. The Sadducees, on the other hand, held rigidly to the Torah and refused to admit any doctrine not expressly contained there. Thus they came to ridicule Jesus' teachings about resurrection by citing a law in Deuteronomy 25:5–6 decreeing that a man should marry his brother's widow in order to guarantee progeny to the family. By imagining an almost absurd instance in which the law would apply, they produced a ridiculous picture of a woman with seven husbands in the resurrection.

Jesus first attempted to correct their vision of resurrected life. Its quality, he said, is quite different from that of this life. In the resurrection, human beings are freed from mundane necessities. They are like the angels, and have no worry about progeny to carry on their names. (Was Jesus also giving the Sadducees a lesson about angels?)

Then he turned on them their own trick of reading the Torah quite literally. Citing Exodus 3:6, when God told Moses, "I am the God of your father, the God of Abraham, the God of Isaac, and the God of Jacob," Jesus observed that there must be a resurrection, else these men could not be living and God could not truly be their God; for God had indeed put it in the present tense, "I *am* the God of your father. . . ."

Some of the scribes, whose business it was to deal in the minutiae of the Law, were obviously much impressed by such an answer. They themselves may have been Pharisees rather than Sadducees. Jesus had proven himself more than a match for any of them.

When they fell silent, he asked them a question. How could they, in the face of Psalm 110:1, where David called the Messiah "Lord," think of the Messiah as David's "son"? The point was, they expected the Messiah, as David's offspring, to have an earthly kingdom like David's. But Jesus was not only David's son, he was his Lord as well, and his Kingdom would transcend the kingdom of David.

Lord, something in me tends to reject subtle arguments that have to do with religion. Is that wrong? I don't want to be fuzzy-minded about my beliefs, but, on the other hand, I don't want to be fussy-minded either. Help me to steer a proper course between wholehearted devotion and sensible belief. In Jesus' name. Amen.

WEEK 10

Week 10: Sunday

Luke 20:45–21:4 A Model for Living

Everywhere in Jerusalem, and especially around the temple, Jesus and the disciples would have seen the figures of the scribes moving through the streets in their long robes with tassels that touched the ground. After the encounter with them recorded in Luke 20:39–44, Jesus commented on these ubiquitous figures to the disciples. They liked to be noticed, he said. They loved the special greetings of "Rabbi" or "Master" which others gave them in the marketplaces and they liked the seats of honor at banquets. Rabbinical writings in fact gave very precise regulations for the seating of scribes, so that the oldest and most authoritative had the greatest places. But in matter of fact, said Jesus, for all their respectability, they used their positions of influence and knowledge of the Law to bilk poor, trusting widows out of their inheritances. And their long prayers, often delivered in public places, were mostly hollow pretense, aimed only at increasing their level of honor among the populace.

How much more appropriate in God's eyes was the behavior of the poor widow Jesus happened to see placing her two small coins in the offering chest at the temple. The coins were not worth much by most people's standards—they were the small Jewish "coppers" which bore no image of Caesar—but they were obviously worth a great deal to the woman, whose appearance marked her as one in very meager circumstances.

In God's eyes, indicated Jesus, she had given more than all the self-important religious people, even though they probably made a great display of dropping their silver denarii into the offering chests. For God looks on the heart of a person, not on the elaborate piety developed for outward show.

Lord, thank you for simple people who are able to love you in simple but profound ways. They help to correct the vision of those of us who are more complicated and less natural. Help me to be more like them. In the name of Jesus, who also gave all that he had. Amen.

Week 10: Monday

Luke 21:5–19 Patterns of Suffering and Hope

Each of the so-called Synoptic Gospels contains a lengthy section of apocalyptic sayings—predictions of Jesus concerning a time of great destruction before the end of the old order and the beginning of the new. In Matthew it is chapter 24. In Mark it is chapter 13. In Luke it is this chapter, chapter 21. Both Matthew and Luke repeat certain material which appeared earlier in Mark. But Luke alone has added material from another source, blending it with the sayings from Mark to form a new apocalypse.

One of the most interesting facts about Luke's finished product is the way he has made the sayings parallel descriptions of Jesus' trial, crucifixion, and resurrection in chapters 22–24. Scholars have long noted the way Luke has developed very intricate parallelisms throughout the Gospel and the Book of Acts as well. But this particular section is greatly illuminated by noting the parallels. Here are some of them:

Chapter 21	*Chapters 22–24*
False Messiahs (v. 8)	Jesus the true Messiah (24:26)
The disciples in prison and before kings and governors (v. 12)	Jesus captured (22:54) and taken before Herod and Pilate (23:1–25)
The disciples betrayed by friends and relatives (v. 16)	Jesus betrayed by Judas (22:47–48)
The disciples hated (v. 17)	Jesus hated (22:63; 23:18, 35–39)
Assurance of God's protection (v. 18)	Jesus' faith in God's protection (23:46)
Endurance demanded of disciples (v. 19)	Jesus shows endurance (22:7–23:46)
Fulfillment of Old Testament (v. 22)	Fulfillment of Old Testament (22: 37; 24:44–46)
Jesus' sorrow for those who have children or expect them (v. 23)	Jesus says the childless are blessed (23:28–29)
The times of the Gentiles (v. 24)	The gospel proclaimed to the Gentiles (24:47)
Signs in the sun (v. 25)	Darkness in the sun (23:44–45)
The coming of the Son of man in glory (v. 27)	The glory of the Son of man at the resurrection (24:26, 46)
Redemption (v. 27)	Jesus, the one to redeem Israel (24:21)

Luke appears to have been saying that the suffering of the disciples would essentially parallel that of Jesus himself, and that they must therefore brace themselves to endure the calamities and hardships as Jesus endured the trial and crucifixion. If they were faithful as he was faithful, they would then share in the glory and triumph of the One who had been resurrected from the dead. And, through it all, the God who raised up Jesus would prove more than adequate to their needs, giving them words to say at their trials and preserving them from harm.

Lord, the pattern of Jesus' suffering, death, and resurrection has been extremely meaningful to me whenever my own spirit has suffered in the human condition. I know there is hope in your power to bring good out of evil and light out of darkness. Grant that I may be more dedicated to spreading the good news of this hope. In Jesus' name. Amen.

Week 10: Tuesday

Luke 21:20–38 When the Summer Is Near

Continuing to weave together verses from Mark and from his other source, Luke here provides a program sketch of how things will happen in the end. First, Jerusalem will be overrun by enemies. Then the whole of nature will erupt and shake the world powers. And finally the Son of man will come in power and glory, bringing redemption for his people.

Jesus frequently alluded to the destruction of Jerusalem. Some scholars think Luke added realistic touches to his description of this destruction when he wrote the Gospel after the actual fall of Jerusalem in A.D. 70. But Jesus' words are similar to those describing the destruction of the city in 586 B.C. and not to the description of the fall in A.D. 70 as depicted by the historian Josephus. He simply foresaw a time of great tribulation for the city that had rejected him. The "times of the Gentiles" (v. 24) seems to allude to chapters 11–12 of the book of Daniel, which describe the clashing of great Gentile armies before the End comes.

Verses 25–26 tell of the age of great natural calamities which will afflict even the Gentile world. The "roaring of the sea and the waves" suggests the temporary eruption of primeval chaos, as the waters which God tamed in the Genesis story of creation rise out of their boundaries and threaten to swallow the land again.

But, in all the disruption and horror, the Son of man will return, "coming in a cloud with power and great glory" (v. 27). Therefore the followers of Jesus should not fear, but should look about them alertly, for their redemption is drawing near. The calamities are like the leaves the fig tree puts out as a sign summer is approaching—they are harbingers of the End.

Verse 32 is admittedly difficult to interpret today. Some think that Jesus firmly expected a precipitous arrival of the End, even before the disciples had died. It seems unlikely, however, that Luke, writing after the fall of Jerusalem, should not have altered this verse when he saw the End being delayed. It is more likely, in the interweaving of sources about the destruction of Jerusalem and the end of the ages, that this particular saying originally applied to the prediction of Jerusalem's fall, not to the End and the return of the Son of man.

The important practical consideration, as verses 34–36 observe, is to live joyously in expectancy of the Kingdom, so that when the time of the End comes, it does not catch us unawares. Having hearts "weighed down with dissipation and drunkenness and cares of this life" is the opposite of living in the mood of ecstasy Luke has so frequently depicted as being appropriate to the Kingdom.

One more note: The other Gospels say that Jesus was spending his nights in the home of Mary, Martha, and Lazarus in the small town of Bethany, about three miles from Jerusalem. Luke says (v. 37) that he was lodging on Mount Olivet. Actually, one must climb Olivet and go beyond it to get to Bethany. Luke may have phrased it this way to impart more meaning to Olivet, as it is both the place of Jesus' retreat to the Garden of Gethsemane (Luke 22:39) and the scene of his ascension (Acts 1:12).

I am often weighed down, O Lord, by the cares of this life. My spirit is depressed by news of violence and greed and upheaval in the world. Sometimes it seems as if the ancient chaos has broken out again. Grant me the faith to watch through it all, living expectantly for the Son of man, who has already been revealed in history. Amen.

Week 10: Wednesday

Luke 22:1–6 A Wicked Agreement

As the day of Passover approached, the Messiah-fever in Jerusalem probably ran higher than ever. The town was garrisoned with soldiers to keep the peace. Jesus was besting the scribes and Pharisees in every discussion in the temple. Excitement was mounting.

The chief priests and scribes were feeling desperate. They knew they must do something—but what? They could not simply arrest Jesus in the daytime. He was far too popular, and there might be reprisals from the crowds. And at night, with the vast throngs milling about the city, it was probably impossible to find him. Until—

Judas became their answer. Judas Iscariot, the dark one, whose life has been largely swallowed up in mystery, except for the perfidy of his betrayal. Why did he do it? The question has been asked thousands of times. There are several possible conclusions. Some think, as John 12:6 indicates, that he had embezzled money from the disciples' common treasury, and needed to cover up his small crime with a larger one. Others believe he was a Zealot, a member of a party of fierce nationalists, and hoped to produce a bloody revolution when Jesus was captured. Still others defend him by suggesting that he may have been merely impatient with Jesus and hoped that the confrontation in the garden would provoke the immediate arrival of the Kingdom. Jesus had, after all, repeatedly spoken of the necessity of his being delivered up and crucified. Perhaps Judas understood this better than the others.

Luke did not trouble with such human alternatives. In his view, the betrayal had theological significance. Judas turned Jesus over to his enemies because Satan had entered into him. Unable to deflect Jesus from his goal of the Kingdom (Luke 4:1–13), Satan found one of the disciples of softer metal, and was working through him to prevent the preaching of the Kingdom.

It was done for money—thirty pieces of silver, says Matthew 26:15, the price of a slave in the Old Testament. After all Jesus' talk about riches—the story of the rich man and Lazarus (Luke 16:19–31), the encounter with the rich ruler who was sad because he could not give up his wealth for the Kingdom (Luke 18:18–30), the joyous meeting with Zacchaeus, the chief tax collector who gave so much of his property to the poor (Luke 19:1–10), the commendation of the poor widow who gave all she had to the temple treasury (Luke 21:1–4)—Judas defected for money. Luke was a doctor. He probably knew many people and had had occasion to witness their actions and emotions in intimate moments. He knew how often economic considerations are the fulcrum on which a person's whole life turns. Again and again, in the Book of Acts, he would note how the greed for money and property was an acid destroying people's lives. It is no wonder that Satan got to one of the disciples through this age-old door.

Lord, I am suddenly fearful of this door in my own life. How ready am I to put economic considerations above everything else—above personal friendships, family values, even my dedication to your Kingdom? I blush, Lord, and pray for forgiveness. Envelop me in your presence until I am safe from Satan's temptings. Through Jesus, who withstood all trials. Amen.

Week 10: Thursday

Luke 22:7–23 Eating the Passover

There was no meal in the entire year more important to Hebrews than the Passover meal. It was like our Fourth of July, Thanksgiving, and Christmas all rolled into one. It was a sacred meal, for it symbolized the birth of the Jewish nation, when a group of slaves in Egypt killed lambs and smeared their blood on the door lintels, so that the death angel spared the Hebrew children when slaying the sons of the Egyptians. But it was also a social meal, the highlight of family life and joy. Even today, it is among Jews a time for remembering the trials and victories of the past, a time for fun and festivity, and a time for considering the hope for the future.

It is much in keeping with Luke's picture of the human, compassionate Jesus that he shows him wanting to eat the Passover one last time with the disciples before he suffered. Other Gospels possibly make more of the theological significance of the Last Supper. Luke obviously sees the human depths of it.

Normally, one ate this meal with members of his family. But we remember that, in his commitment to the Kingdom, Jesus had said that his followers had become his family (Luke 8:19–21). Similarly, he had told the disciples that he must come first with them, even before their fathers and mothers and wives and children and brothers and sisters (Luke 14:25–26). Thus they had established a precedent to be remembered always in the Christian fellowship, especially at the time of communion—that the followers of the Lord are a special family together, transcending even the relationships among family members.

It seems strange that Luke has reversed the order of the bread and the cup, putting the sharing of the cup ahead of the breaking of the bread. A similar order is suggested, however, in 1 Corinthians 10:16–21 and in a second-century book of teachings for the church called the *Didachē*. It may be that both orders existed side by side in the early church. The symbolism of this one would actually be more precise than the one given in Mark 14:22–25 and 1 Corinthians 11:23–27, because Jesus' blood was spilled before his body was taken down in broken form.

Verses 21–23 refer of course to the betrayal by Judas. But the key words are in verse 22: "as it has been determined." Luke was invariably concerned to point out that everything that happened in Jesus' life and suffering had been prophesied and foreordained by God. Even the betrayal itself was assimilated into the divine plan and purpose.

> *Lord, I think of my mother-in-law eating her last Thanksgiving meal with us, and knowing it was her last. How much it meant to her! And how much this Passover meal must have meant to Jesus, who loved Israel as no man except the Son of God could have loved her. How the joy and sadness must have mingled in his heart that night! Help me to remember this strong personal emotion when I receive the cup and the bread and join with him in the prayer for the great banquet to come in the Kingdom.* Amen.

Luke 22:24–38 The Way of the Kingdom

There is a kind of sadness in these verses. Jesus has been with the disciples for months, instructing them, sharing himself with them, modeling ministry for them. Yet they are still like children who cannot understand.

They are still like the scribes and Pharisees, who love to have the best places at the table (Luke 11:43; 20:46), and they fall to arguing about it, possibly after a bit too much wine to drink. Jesus reminds them that the Kingdom ideal is to serve, not to be served. As Father Louis Evely has reminded us, we come to the table to serve him, but he always puts on the apron and serves us.

If the disciples will maintain this posture of obedient service, then they will become the pillars of the new Israel, the leaders of the twelve tribes of the blessed! But they will not do so without interruption. First, they will all fall away—even Simon Peter, who thinks he is ready to go to prison and the grave for his Master. As Satan entered Judas, he has also demanded to try Peter. But Jesus has prayed for him, and Satan will not be able to keep him.

Verses 35–38 are a word of warning to the disciples. When Jesus sent them out before, they were able to live off the hospitality of others wherever they went. But shortly, when Jesus has been crucified and his name maligned throughout the land, they will find the going much harder. Doors will then be shut to them that were open before. They will find it necessary to carry provisions, and even to go about armed for self-protection. Jesus will be known as a transgressor, a criminal, and they will be labeled as his accomplices. Taking him quite literally, the disciples produce two swords. "It is enough," he says—meaning probably to let the matter go, they have said enough about it.

Lord, I want to serve you. But my spirit is unruly, especially when those I am to wait upon are slick and arrogant and undeserving. Then I want to be a ruler, not a servant. Help me to remember you in the

Passion, and humbly take my place beside you. For it is the way of the Kingdom. Amen.

Week 10: Saturday

Luke 22:39–46 The Custom of Praying

Luke alone, among the Gospel writers, records that it was Jesus' *custom* to go to the Mount of Olives to pray. Were it not for this, we might suppose that this experience on the night of the Passover was an isolated incident. But apparently it was not. Each evening throughout the week, as Jesus and the disciples returned from the temple to the place of their lodging, they stopped here to commune with God, to feel the presence that recomposed their minds and restored their energies.

Mark in his Gospel (14:26–42) was more interested in the disciples' failure to understand the cruciality of the hour and to pray than he was in the agony of Jesus. But not so Luke! Unlike both Mark and Matthew, he does not record how Jesus three times returned and found the disciples asleep when they should have been praying. Instead, he describes, as they do not, the manner of Jesus' personal anguish—how a heavenly messenger appeared to strengthen him in his praying, as one would be joined in a mighty task by an ethereal stranger, and how the very pores of his body exuded drops of blood because of the enormous stress and intensity of the prayer.

Luke wished us to see, without question, the terrible human struggle going on in Jesus as the devil made a last mighty effort to deter him from purchasing a Kingdom through his own suffering and death.

Lord, I am grateful for this warm, poignant picture of Jesus struggling through prayer with the destiny he knew was coming. It enables me to enter my own times of crisis-praying with more courage and confidence, for I see that the important outcome is not release from suffering but submission to your will. Amen.

WEEK 11

Week 11: Sunday

Luke 22:47–53 The Power of Darkness

Professor Harry Levin of Harvard University once wrote a book called *The Power of Blackness.* It was a critical study of the fiction of Hawthorne, Melville, and Poe, designed to reveal how the inordinate power of their writing derived at least in part from their ability to tap the dark side of events and the world. The phrase with which Luke ended this passage is similar to Professor Levin's title, for Luke, even more than Professor Levin, appreciated the way evil forces are at work in the world we live in.

Here, the evil triumph comes as the culmination of many battles with Jesus throughout his ministry. The devil never managed to touch Jesus himself in a vulnerable spot, but he had reached to the heart of Judas, one of his disciples. And he was using the religious establishment of Jerusalem—the chief priests, scribes, and Pharisees—as a veritable phalanx to move against Jesus. Here they were, massed together with torches, knives, and clubs, closing in on the Master at his place of prayer. Judas had been with him when he stopped there on preceding evenings, and so knew precisely where to lead the others to capture him.

The disciples had already alluded to the two swords they had among them (Luke 22:38). They are ready to defend their Master, and one (we know from John 18:10 that it is Simon Peter) even strikes off the ear of one of the enemy. But Jesus has already decreed that his Kingdom is not to be won as an ordinary kingdom and, healing the severed ear, bids the disciples not to offer resistance. He is, after all, no common criminal, that they should come for him with staves and swords. Their matter with him must be tried in the courts, not on the field of battle.

Perhaps the saddest note of all is in verses 47–48. It was the custom for rabbis and their followers to greet each other with a kiss. But Jesus, knowing what Judas had conspired to do, was unwilling to have him add to his perfidy the hypocrisy of a kiss.

It was indeed the enemies' hour—and Satan's. But Jesus' hour would come.

Lord, it has been said that the brave man murders with a sword, the coward with a kiss. How many times, I wonder, have I betrayed you with a kiss, saying the pious word, pretending a righteous gesture, acting as if I were on your side, when in fact I was weakly committed to you, if at all. Give me the courage to be honest in the expression of my feelings; and, even more, give me the grace to love you devotedly. Through Jesus, who refused a kiss that wasn't meant. Amen.

Week 11: Monday

Luke 22:54–65 A Bitter Reminder

In Mark's account of this part of the Gospel, Jesus was taken immediately before the Sanhedrin for trial, and Peter's denial occurred in the courtyard outside while the trial was going on. Luke's account, which is more probable, has Jesus being held in the courtyard of the high priest's house until morning, when he was brought to the Sanhedrin. This means that Peter was very close to where Jesus was being mocked and beaten by the soldiers—perhaps only a few yards away, in full view of it all—and that Jesus could hear each of his denials.

The courtyard would not have been large—perhaps sixty by seventy feet. The fire would have been lit for warmth as well as light, for the early spring nights are frosty in Israel. Peter showed a certain courage in entering the courtyard and then in staying after the scrutiny of a maid first identified him as one of Jesus' followers. But the courage did not run deep enough. Three times he denied that he had been with Jesus. And then, the third time, before the words had died on his lips, the cock crowed. Jesus, who all through the night had been the object of ridicule and mistreatment by men who were holding him for the dawn, heard it too, and looked at Peter. Their eyes met, and Peter remembered.

What could he do? He remembered all the good days together—how proud he had been to be the first of the disciples during the months of triumph and popularity—"and he went out and wept bitterly."

Lord, this is the saddest passage. I know how Peter felt in the courtyard—and how he felt when he realized he had betrayed a friend who loved him. But thank you for the story. It reminds us that we can return to faithfulness even after we have disappointed you. Help me to be faithful. Through Jesus, who prays for his own. Amen.

Week 11: Tuesday

Luke 22:66–71 Jesus and the Old Men

The assembly of elders was comprised of priests, scribes, Pharisees, and Sadducees, representing the main power blocs in Jewish life. As in other occupied countries, the Roman government allowed the local assembly to transact most of the business affecting their nations's internal affairs.

We can picture the assembly as it met on that fateful morning. The members were not all evil men. Many were persons of deep conscience and moral conviction. They were like the members of any court or tribunal, who must live with their own personal, business, and family problems at the same time that they take the bench and make decisions affecting others. They simply did not know all the facts in the case, and did not fully understand what they were doing.

They wanted to hear only one thing from Jesus—did he think he was the Messiah? "Why should I tell you?" Jesus replied, in effect. "If I did, you would not believe me. And if I question you—if I pose the evidence for you and ask you about it, as I have in the past—you will not answer, but merely become silent."

But he did tell them one thing—that from then on the Son of man would be seated at God's right hand, enthroned in power. His hour of glory had come. Satan's dominion would be shaken.

"Are you the Son of God, then"—the Messiah? they asked. Mark says that he replied, "I am" (Mark 14:62). But both Matthew and Luke have altered the account to read "You have said so" (Matt. 26:64) or "You say that I am" (Luke 22:70), as though Jesus were simply resigning the matter, and implying, "Think what you will."

At any rate, the elders accepted this as an admission of his claim to be the Messiah and bound him over to Pilate's jurisdiction. Their own charge against him was theological, that he was guilty of blasphemy; but the charge on which they would present him to Pilate was political, that he was guilty of sedition.

We can only wonder how many of the council members felt uneasy at going along with the majority in this condemnation. We know from Luke 23:50–51 that at least one, Joseph of Arimathea, was not in agreement with the decision. How many of them suspected that they had been pressured into a verdict wanted by a few leaders, and wished they had had no part in it?

To be human, O Lord, is to be involved in a network of complicity and guilt from which there is never complete extrication. We all make decisions—sometimes wrong ones—affecting the lives and destinies of others. Help me to be sensitive to this, and always to have the courage to act honestly and compassionately in matters involving others. Through Jesus, who suffered the greatest injustice at the hands of "good" men. Amen.

Week 11: Wednesday

Luke 23:1–12 A Basis for Friendship

It is unlikely that the assembly of elders had the power to order the death penalty for Jesus. Even if they had it, however, they probably preferred that the Roman governor be the one to pass sentence in a case so volatile as this one. So all of them—those opposed to the decision as well as those for it—came clattering into Pilate's hall to hear the matter prosecuted there.

The three accusations in verse 2 are all related to the charge of sedition—Jesus was stirring up the people, he had advised the crowds not to pay the annual poll tax, and he proclaimed himself to be a Messiah-King. The first two charges were absolutely false. Jesus had consistently refused to excite the populace about his messiahship, and had attempted to keep it secret. The agents for the chief priests and scribes had tried to get him to say that the people should not pay taxes to Caesar, but he had not been caught in their trap (Luke 20:20–26). And we have seen in Luke 22:66–71 how the assembly drew from him the admission—if indeed it was an admission—that he was the Messiah. But the Sanhedrin was not after truth in this matter, but action. It translated everything into a language it believed would move Pilate to do as they wished.

Pilate attempted to understand the matter as well as he could. "Are you the King of the Jews?" he asked Jesus. "Are you trying to start an insurrection in Jerusalem?" Jesus remained quiet and dignified, knowing that no direct answer from him would avail against the entire council of old men. Pilate said he seemed innocent enough to him. But the Sanhedrin declared that he was going throughout the country, from Galilee to Judea, stirring up the populace.

The mention of Galilee gave Pilate the out he needed. Learning that Jesus was indeed a Galilean, he declared that Herod should have jurisdiction in the matter, for Herod was the tetrarch of Galilee. It would be a good move, Pilate thought, to cement relations that had not been good in the past. It would please Herod—perhaps win him over.

Herod, we recall, had long been interested in Jesus. He had wondered if he were John the Baptist come back to life (Luke 9:7–9), and had tried to see him. Now his curiosity would be fulfilled!

But Jesus was no more talkative before Herod than he had been before the Sanhedrin or Pilate. So, after some mockery and buffoonery at Jesus' expense, Herod's soldiers arrayed Jesus in a fancy robe, as if he were indeed a king, and sent him back to Pilate. The occasion became the basis for a new friendship between the two rulers, and we can imagine their talking about Jesus at some subsequent banquet.

Verse 10 is a vivid parenthesis depicting the venomous activity of some of the council members—they were a rabble of accusers, spitting and hissing like a nest of vipers!

Lord, I pray for every innocent person who must bear this kind of treatment today from authorities in the law or government. Give him or her the grace to behave with inner composure as Jesus did, that the indignities may not wound deeply. And hasten the full coming of your Kingdom, that all people may dwell together as brothers and sisters with mutual respect. Amen.

Luke 23:13–25 The Master and a Murderer

The goddess Justice is usually pictured wearing a blindfold. This is meant to emphasize her impartiality in rendering judgments. But our experiences in life suggest that it might also be interpreted as a sign of her ineptness, her blindness to the facts that would really make for justice.

The story of Barabbas's release fits the latter interpretation better than the former. Ironically, Barabbas was in prison for precisely the same charges as those for which the priests and elders had arraigned Jesus before Pilate—sedition and insurrection. Yet, despite Jesus' innocence of the charges, they shouted vehemently for Barabbas's release and Jesus' crucifixion!

Verse 17, which has been omitted from the RSV translation because it is missing from the oldest, most reliable texts of the Gospel of Luke, is necessary to explain Pilate's action. The Romans, as a mark of favor to the Jews, had a practice of releasing a political prisoner of their choice during the festival time (cf. Mark 15:6). Therefore, when Pilate said that he had found Jesus innocent of the charges made against him, and that Herod, one of their own rulers, had found him innocent as well, and would consequently release him, they all set up a clamor to have Barabbas released but to have Jesus put to death.

If we had only Luke's account to reckon from, we would wonder what had happened among the populace to destroy the favor in which they had so recently held Jesus. But Mark 15:11 informs us that "the chief priests stirred up the crowd" to have Pilate release Barabbas instead of Jesus. We can imagine, when Luke says "they were urgent, demanding with loud cries" that Jesus should be crucified, that the priests and elders were among those crying the loudest. Clever people that they were, they incited the crowd to do their evil work for them.

Lord, it is a fearful responsibility to be a leader of any kind. I pray for those who have roles of leadership today, especially in the world community. Grant to them a fierce respect for human rights and justice, so that they always put the good of others ahead of their own self-interest. In Jesus' name. Amen.

Week 11: Friday

Luke 23:26–31 The Crying of the Women

Simon of Cyrene is one of those special people who, by happening to be at a particular place in a given moment, are cast by unexpected circumstances into the spotlight of history. We know almost nothing about him—he may have been a Jewish pilgrim arriving in Jerusalem after taking the Passover with relatives or friends in the country, or he may have been a one-time inhabitant of Cyrene now living near Jerusalem—but he has since become the subject of hundreds of paintings, poems, and sermons. The cross the soldiers ordered him to carry behind Jesus was the cross bar—not an entire cross—which would be hoisted and affixed to an upright pole or a kind of scaffolding at the scene of execution.

The women who followed with the crowd had commenced the funeral custom of loud public mourning even in advance of Jesus' death. Apparently they were not the same women who had accompanied him as disciples (Luke 8:1–3), but local residents, as he called them "daughters of Jerusalem." Jesus was not angry with them; he merely used their wailing as the basis for a prophetic warning about the future destruction of the city by the Romans. It was considered accursed for a women to remain barren and have no children. But Jesus reversed that popular standard, saying that in the day of catastrophe it would be the barren ones who would be thought blessed, for they would not have to witness the cruel slaughter of their children. If a miscarriage of justice such as one resulting in Jesus' death could occur under present relatively calm conditions, what would happen in that time of national disaster?

Of course, Jesus was right. Descriptions of the sacking and destruction of a city under seige are among the most horrifying accounts in all history, and the Roman demolition of Jerusalem would have offered no exception. The people of Jerusalem bought no favor with anyone by their failure to rise up in support of Jesus. Evil simply increased its hold on them until, a few years later, their beloved city was mercilessly destroyed.

Lord, I understand the feelings of the women of Jerusalem. They were helpless against the will of those in power. Teach me to listen to the voices of those who are powerless, that I may more often know what justice is. Through Jesus, who is on the side of the little ones. Amen.

Week 11: Saturday

Luke 23:32–43 Paradise in the Wilderness

For centuries, preachers have delivered series of sermons on such topics as "Faces Around the Cross," "Attitudes at Calvary," and "Choosing Sides at the Foot of the Cross." It is no wonder, for there is a marvelous spectrum of points of view and ways of behaving represented in this single passage of scripture.

First, there is the way of Jesus himself—regal, quietly confident, and forgiving of those who did not understand how Satan was using them as pawns and dupes in his last great bid for supremacy. It is one thing to be a king when the sun is shining and everything is going in your favor; it is quite another thing when everything is going against you, as it seemed to be for Jesus.

Then there was the way of the crowd. They stood "watching," says Luke. They were not sure what would happen. Suppose he really were the Messiah—would the Kingdom come as he hung upon the cross? Perhaps some among the crowd had shouted for the crucifixion hoping that it might be so.

And there was the way of the rulers—the priests and scribes and other elders of the city. They scoffed at Jesus, trying to convince the people once and for all that he was no messiah. "There are many reports of his saving others," they say—"all the way from Galilee to here in the temple. He healed and raised people from the dead. All right, if he is truly the Messiah, let him help himself now. That will prove his case."

What they didn't see, of course, and had never been able to see, was that his whole messiahship was of another order, a wholly unselfish order, than the one they envisioned for Israel. From the beginning, he had rejected the devil's offer of an easy kingdom and popularity for himself. His Kingdom was for the outcasts—the poor, infirm, blind, and oppressed. It was for the captive, like the poor criminal dying beside him, who asked to be remembered.

Even among the criminals crucified with Jesus there were two attitudes. One was like that of the rulers—rude, impertinent, mocking. But the other was that of a sober man who, even in the extremity of his dying, did not lose touch with the facts before him. Jesus was no criminal as they were. He was being put to death as "The King of the Jews"—a title both true and satirical at the same time.

"Remember me," asked the man, "when you come in your kingly power" (v. 42,P).

What did he know about Jesus? How much did he understand about the Kingdom? Clearly, at least, he understood more than the rulers of Israel who were crucifying Jesus—he understood that the Kingdom was for prostitutes and tax collectors, lost sheep and wayward sons, Samaritan pilgrims and penitent thieves—he understood that it was for him!

And Jesus, with the note of authority that had always characterized his ministry, said to him, "Today"—not tomorrow or at some future date when the Kingdom has fully come—"today you will be with me in Paradise." Paradise. The Aramaic word he used was from an old Persian word, *pardes*, meaning "garden." To the Jewish mind, it spoke both of the Garden of Eden and of the heavenly abode of God, where no evil existed but all was made innocent again in the divine presence. The criminal who believed would go from the cross to the Kingdom, from the wilderness to the garden, that very day.

Lord, how easy it is to sit here and take the right side in this story as I read it. But how hard it often is to take the right side when you are being crucified in the world today. Often I take the wrong side and only recognize afterwards that it was you being put to death in that legislative bill, in that election referendum, in that zoning decision, in that school classroom, in that dispute I overheard in the grocery store. Make me far more sensitive, Lord, to the way you are treated in the world around me, that I may not end up on the side of the mockers. Amen.

WEEK 12

Week 12: Sunday

Luke 23:44–49 Signs, Portents, and Sadness

Ancient peoples—and some not so ancient—believed that signs in nature often corroborated certain key events in human life and history. Passages in Amos (8:9) and Joel (2:10, 31; 3:15) connected such signs with the Day of the Lord. However literally or figuratively one wishes to construe verse 44, there could be no more fitting natural symbol for the death of the Messiah than that the sun, the center of the universe, blushed and hid its face at the shame of what was done.

The curtain alluded to in verse 45 was the great veil separating the outer part of the temple, where daily worship was performed, from the inner part, or Holy of Holies, where only the high priest entered and offered sacrifice once each year, on the Day of Atonement. Great fear was attached to this yearly entrance, for God's presence was believed to be concentrated especially in the Holy of Holies. A rope was even tied around the high priest's ankle, so that, in the event he suffered a heart attack and died there, becoming accursed, his body could be retrieved by the priests and people waiting outside. The legend among the Christians that the curtain had been torn in two was a dramatic symbol of the end of the priestly system or religion and the new freedom of all persons, including the unclean, to enter into the presence of God.

Jesus' final words, like so many others he spoke from the cross, are from the Psalms, and remind us once more of the importance of steeping ourselves in the great devotional literature of our faith. They are from Psalm 31:5, and are set in a context expressing strong assurance in God's care and delivery for the person beset by suffering.

> Yea, thou art my rock and my fortress;
> for thy name's sake lead me and guide me,
> take me out of the net which is hidden for me,
> for thou art my refuge.
> Into thy hand I commit my spirit;
> thou hast redeemed me, O Lord, faithful God.
> Psalm 31:3–5

Mark 15:39 says that the centurion, when Jesus had died, declared that he was truly the Son of God. Apparently it suited Luke's purposes of apologetic better to interpret his remark as a testimony to Jesus' innocence. This would have been important to a Roman audience, as it confirmed what Pilate, the Roman governor, had already decided (Luke 23:4, 13–16).

Luke alone records the information in verse 48 about the crowd's returning home in a mood of lamentation and penitence. Taken together with verse 35, which says they were "watching" the crucifixion in an attitude unlike that of the rulers, who scoffed and mocked, it indicates that the people were generally convinced that injustice had prevailed and Jesus was a good man. Even if they were not sure he was the Messiah, they knew a prophet and wonder-worker had been put to death that day.

And there is a mellow sadness in verse 49, which says that all of those who had followed him from Galilee "stood at a distance" and saw everything that happened. If Jesus could have spoken to them from the cross, perhaps he would have quoted to them the last verse of Psalm 31—verse 5—which he had cited in dying. It says:

> Be strong, and let your heart take courage,
> all you who wait for the Lord!
>
> Psalm 31:24

Lord, sometimes I wish the curtain in the temple were still there. It is such a responsibility to have your holy presence meeting me everywhere I turn. You are there in my morning shower, in the meal I eat, in the person I speak to, in the game I play with the children, in the way I do my work. Give me courage, Lord, not only to wait for you, but to meet you where you already are! In Jesus' name. Amen.

Week 12: Monday

Luke 23:50–56 An Act of Restitution

How many times in life the only thing we can do is to try in some small way to make amends for the wrong that has been done to another—to put an arm around the student who has been unfairly treated by fellow students or a teacher, to invite to dinner an employee who has been unjustly fired, to treat generously the victim of racial prejudice or social inequity. It does not undo the wrong or compensate in any way for the sacrilege committed. But it is all we can do, in our feeble manner, to reach out and say, "I am sorry, I wish it hadn't happened."

This is essentially what Joseph of Arimathea did in caring for the body of Jesus. Matthew 27:57 and John 19:38 say that Joseph was "a disciple of Jesus." Luke is more concerned to stress his humanitarian quality, his honest resistance to the Sanhedrin's "purpose and deed," and his basic Jewish hope in the Kingdom of

God. His act took some courage in the face of Pharisaic piety and the laws about touching the dead, who were considered unclean, and in Jesus' case, accursed as well. The tomb may have been his own, in which case the devotion shown would be similar to that of the woman in Mark 14:3–9 who anointed Jesus' head with her own expensive burial perfume. It was his way of saying he was sorry, that Jesus had not deserved such treatment as he had received.

While Joseph was taking the body to the tomb, the Galilean women followed—perhaps they performed traditional mourning rites along the way—and saw where it was buried. Then, returning to the marketplace, they purchased spices and ointments for anointing the body, and retired to their lodging places as the sun was setting, to wait through the sabbath day and come again to the tomb.

Lord, what a long day it must have been through which the women waited! I pray for all of those who wait now for their return to the grave where a loved one has just been buried. The hours drag for them too. Let them discover in this heavy time the hope that we have through him who was laid in a borrowed tomb, yet could not be held by death. Amen.

Week 12: Tuesday

Luke 24:1–12 A Throwaway Scene

The Gospel of Mark's account of the empty tomb contains some significant differences from Luke's: It has a single messenger at the tomb (Mark 16:5), not two (Luke 24:4); the messenger tells the women that Jesus has gone ahead of them to Galilee (Mark 16:7), instead of reminding them of what Jesus said to them in Galilee (Luke 24:6–7); the women are afraid and tell no one what they have found (Mark 16:8), instead of telling the others what they have seen and not being believed (Luke 24:10–11).

It accorded with Mark's themes and theology to end his Gospel with the women's fear and silence. But how does Luke's interpretation of this final event fit into his overall message? As Mark's narrative of the life and ministry of Jesus focused on its strange power and the disciples' inability to grasp its meaning, Luke's has centered on the theme of the great joy that has come to those who received the Kingdom. Thus this passage serves as a mere prelude to the joy experienced by the disciples from Emmaus when Jesus eats with them (Luke 24:28–32) and by the followers when they realize what has taken place (Luke 24:52). In dramatic terms, it is a "throwaway" scene—one that sacrifices any particular significance of its own to the building of plot and intrigue further on in the play.

The women find the tomb empty and are reminded that Jesus told them he must die but would not be held by the grave. Then they go to report this to all the other followers—but are not believed. It is the negative moment from which the joyous, positive ones will soon follow.

Lord, help me to recognize the throwaway scenes in my own life—those whose significance lies in what is about to happen—and thus to give thanks for those otherwise negative or less exciting times and wait in humble expectancy for what will be revealed. Through Jesus, who sanctifies all time, even the time when little seems to occur. Amen.

Week 12: Wednesday

Luke 24:13–35 A Remarkable Visitor

Luke alone, of the Gospel writers, has preserved this lovely story of the two disciples who were returning home in dejection and then were left in elation when they realized who had visited with them along the way. Very probably they had been among Jesus' acquaintances who had "stood at a distance" and observed the crucifixion (Luke 23:49). As traveling would have been forbidden after sundown on the day of crucifixion, because that was the beginning of the sabbath, they would have had to remain in Jerusalem over the sabbath. They were walking homeward the day after when Jesus approached them on the road and began walking with them.

We have normally thought of the two disciples as being two men, for the Greek word in verse 25 is masculine in form and is translated "O fools" (KJV) or "O foolish men" (RSV). But there is nothing in the Greek form to forbid the possibility that the two disciples were a man and a woman. In fact, considering the fact that they lived together, it seems probable that they were.

At any rate, Jesus gave the two persons an extended lesson in Old Testament prophecy. He showed them that the entire pattern of Hebrew thought should have pointed the Jews to understand Israel's mission in terms of suffering and servanthood; if they had only seen this, they would not have been put off by his death, for only by suffering could he enter the kind of glory God intended for him.

It would have been meaningful to early Christians that the two followers recognized Jesus in the breaking of bread *after* the long lesson in Old Testament prophecies. This pattern was not unlike that of their own worship—first having the Scriptures explained and then meeting the risen Lord in the eucharistic meal.

Jesus' vanishing out of their sight is in keeping with the nature of beatific visions. Our earthly psyches are too fragile to sustain such visitations for very long. We must return to our normal mode of existence. But our awareness of life is greatly heightened by such rare experiences.

Verse 32 speaks of the unusual sense of joy the two disciples felt even before they recognized who their strange visitor was, and it was in this mood of ecstasy that they retraced their way to Jerusalem that very hour—in the dark!—and found the eleven to tell them what had happened. The eleven were not entirely surprised, for Simon Peter had already had a similar visitation and reported it.

The Resurrection clearly meant one thing: Jesus was no longer confined by normal restrictions of time and space in which mortal lives are framed, but was free to appear wherever and whenever he pleased, to this disciple and that, in this place and another.

How often, Lord, you probably walk with me in my way and I do not recognize you. Forgive me for my lack of perception, and help me, through careful study of the Scriptures and a life of prayerful reflection, to discern your presence more regularly. Your only limits are the ones I impose upon you. Amen.

Week 12: Thursday

Luke 24:36–43 The Spirit Who Ate Fish

We are like the disciples in this passage. Our views about reality are largely set by the society around us and what it has taught us to expect. Therefore, even if Jesus were to appear to us as he did to the disciples, we would believe him to be an hallucination of some kind, not a real flesh-and-blood person.

It was especially important, in the early church, to emphasize that the resurrected Jesus was truly corporeal and not a mere phantom. There was a heretical form of the faith, called Docetism, which maintained that Christ's spirit came into his flesh at birth and forsook it at death. This was counter to the teaching of full incarnationism, which maintained that Jesus was resurrected in body, not merely in spirit. Luke was here trying to enforce correct belief. The Gospel of John, which is believed to have been written as a defense against the Docetists, contains similar stories emphasizing the true bodily nature of the resurrected Jesus (cf. John 20:24–29; 21:1–14).

Jesus invited the disciples to touch him and handle him—to know him nonverbally. It was a marvelous invitation, for it is quite possible that our deepest "knowings" are tactile rather than aural or intellectual. Ashley Montagu, in his classic study *Touching,* says that the act of touching and being touched when we are infants is the most important assurance we ever have of our parents' love and our well-being in life. Jesus wanted the disciples to be satisfied in the most basic way possible that it was really he who stood before them. He even took fish and ate it to show them he was no ghost. He was a vital, living person.

The phrase Luke used in verse 41, "they still disbelieved for joy," is characteristic of his thrust in the Gospel. This that had come to pass was simply too great to believe! Nothing in the disciples' experience of life had fully prepared them for it. They could only shake their heads in wonder at the outcome.

Lord, I become excited merely reading about the disciples' great joy. How could the church become so lethargic and apathetic in the wake of such a report? Help me to be open to the same "disbelief of joy" in my own life. Through him who is the cause for such joy, Jesus our Lord. Amen.

Week 12: Friday

Luke 24:44–49 The Charging of Witnesses

The disciples took seriously Jesus' charge to be witnesses to all they had seen and heard of his ministry, death, and resurrection. Later, as recorded in Acts 10:39–41, Peter declared to Cornelius, the man who sought his help for the Gentiles: "We are witnesses to all that he did both in the country of the Jews and in Jerusalem. They put him to death by hanging him on a tree; but God raised him on the third day and made him manifest; not to all the people but to us who were chosen by God as witnesses, who ate and drank with him after he rose from the dead."

The Old Testament is full of references to witnesses. Usually the word had a legal sense, as of those who testified to the truth of a matter. But perhaps the most significant ancient prototype for the Christian witness is to be found in Isaiah 43:10—

> "You are my witnesses," says the Lord,
> "and my servant whom I have chosen,
> that you may know and believe me
> and understand that I am He."

This entire chapter of Isaiah is set in the councils of heaven, which operate as a law court for the nations. The prophet describes God's intention of saving Israel and gathering up her offspring from the east, west, north, and south, that they may testify that he is God.

Jesus' disciples were commissioned to be witnesses of the new Israel, the spiritual community God would gather from the four corners of the world. They would begin in Jerusalem, but eventually their message would go out to all the nations. The "promise" of the Father was of a great people, as had been pledged to Abraham centuries before (Gen. 12:1–3), and the fulfilling of the promise would bring the "great joy" of which the angels had spoken to the shepherds when Christ was born (Luke 2:10–11).

Ironically, perhaps, the Greek word translated "witness" is *martus*, from which we derive the word *martyr.* In making their faithful witness, many of the disciples would suffer or lose their lives, for the evil one would not give up his world without a struggle. But the joy was never diminished by this. It was like a lamp whose wick was always trimmed and made to burn even brighter by slander and persecution.

Lord, in my way I am a witness too, for I have heard and seen things of the Kingdom. Make me daily more conscious of this, that I may give my testimony to others. Clothe me with power as you did the disciples, and use me in the fulfilling of your promise. Through Jesus, who will be Lord of lords and King of kings. Amen.

Luke 24:50–53 The Blessing and the Joy

Before Moses died at the edge of the promised land, he raised his hands and pronounced a blessing over the tribes of Israel (Deut. 33). Near the end of the blessing, he said these words:

> Happy are you, O Israel! Who is like you,
> a people saved by the Lord,
> the shield of your help,
> and the sword of your triumph!
> Deuteronomy 33:29

Jesus may have spoken similar words to the disciples when he blessed them before leaving them. He had gone with them on the road as far as Bethany, which took them over the Mount of Olives where they had been praying the night Judas led the enemy to him. Some ancient manuscripts add to verse 51 the words "and was carried up into heaven," which would accord well with references in Acts to his ascension (Acts 1:2, 9–11). But Luke may originally have omitted such a reference here, preferring to picture Jesus as being on the road to somewhere. Indeed, that is where the disciples would often find him as they traveled with the gospel—he would appear to them in this place and that, as he had to the ones going to Emmaus, and strengthen them for the task he had given them.

However it was, he blessed them and left them, and they returned to Jerusalem to worship in the temple and wait for the outpouring of God's power. Mark, it will be recalled, represented Jesus as ordering the disciples immediately to Galilee (Mark 16:7), where they would see him. Jerusalem, in Mark, stands for all that is evil and arrayed against Jesus; Jesus abandons it for the place where his ministry was successful. But Luke sees a different symbolism in the city—he remembers the prophecies that picture it as the center of God's renewing activity in the world (cf. Isa. 35:8–10).

Therefore he has the disciples return to the city and the temple, where the stage is set for the descent of the Spirit in Acts 2 and the beginnings of a vast missionary enterprise that will eventually carry the gospel into all the world.

The Gospel ends on the note that has been so characteristic of it all along—on the "great joy" of those who have seen what God is doing and have become a part of it. It has been a Gospel of angels' songs, great feasts, stories of glad returns, excitement about healings and resurrections, and the ecstasy of those who have recognized the arrival of the Kingdom of God. No wonder the last words are that they "were continually in the temple blessing God!"

Lord, this whole Gospel has accused me of being far less joyous and excited about your Kingdom than I have every right to be. Teach me to set my days in the light of your presence, that they may become storehouses of delight, and to see the world as the arena of your great victory, that I may hope even in the face of despair. Through Jesus, who blesses me and helps me to worship. Amen.